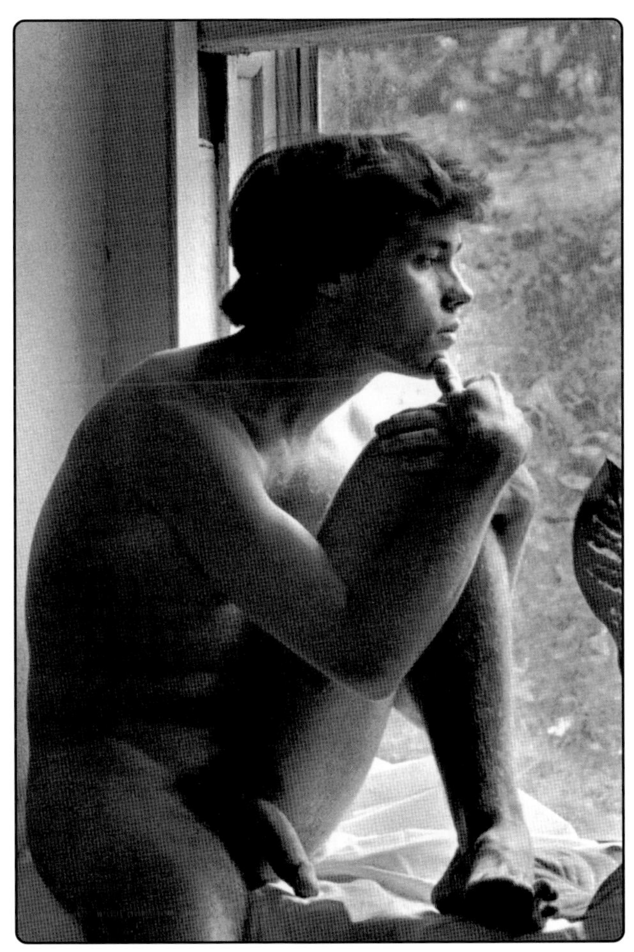

Self-portrait   *1980*

Acknowledgment

I owe a tremendous debt to the men who have appeared in this publication. Guys, thank you for your time, your patience and your participation in this project. I hope you agree with me that the shaving, the posing, the cold, the sunburns and the fireworks were all worth it. For helping me to locate and convince these wonderful men to model, I owe a special thanks to Tom Spaccarelli, David Bearden and Lem Suiter.

Props and good locations can be hard to find. For their hospitality and generosity in providing both, I am forever indebted to Sanford McGee, Sopon Geramethakul, Angela Kinney, Cissy Webb, Oscar Hernandez, Bill Geoffrion, Bobby Dolehide, Schon Oppert, Bogdan Zmidzinski, Jeff Prince and Zbigniew Kantorosinski.

David Maya and Angela Kinney provided me with the motivation to put down the camera long enough to seek out a publisher. Thank you both for pushing me to take that step.

Over the years, the staff at Asman Photo in Washington, D.C. have seen me more often than some of my closest friends and family members. I appreciate the care they have always taken with my work and especially the beautiful job they have done with the final archival images for this book.

I wish to thank José Villarrubia for writing the introduction for *Totems of Desire*, for helping me select which images to submit and for photographing me for this publication. Likewise, I thank Aubrey Walter for his encouragement and support through his editing and publication of this collection of my photographs. Collaborating with the two of you on this edition has been an enriching experience and a true pleasure.

I dedicate this book to Thompson Yee for his unconditional love and years of support. I acknowledge and honor the contributions that he has made to my life, my work and my vision of the world.

Fehl Cannon
Washington, D.C., 2001

First published 2001 by Éditions Aubrey Walter,
Heretic Books Ltd, 27 Old Gloucester Street,
London WC1N 3XX, England
email: aubrey@gmppubs.co.uk   web site: **www.gmppubs.co.uk**
This collection world copyright © 2001 Éditions Aubrey Walter,
Heretic Books Ltd
Individual images world copyright © 2001 Fehl Cannon
Introduction world copyright © 2001 José Villarrubia

Distributed in Europe by
Central Books Ltd,
99 Wallis Road, London, E9 5LN, England
Fax +44 181 533 5821 Phone +44 181 986 4854

Distributed in North America by
LPC Group,
1436 West Randolph Street, Chicago, IL 60607, U S A
Fax +1 312 432 7601 Phone +1 312 432 7650

Distributed in Australia & New Zealand by
Bulldog Books,
P O Box 300, Beaconsfield, NSW 2014, Australia
Fax +61 2 9699 3527 Phone +61 2 9699 3507

Designed and packaged in EU
Reproduced and printed in Hong Kong

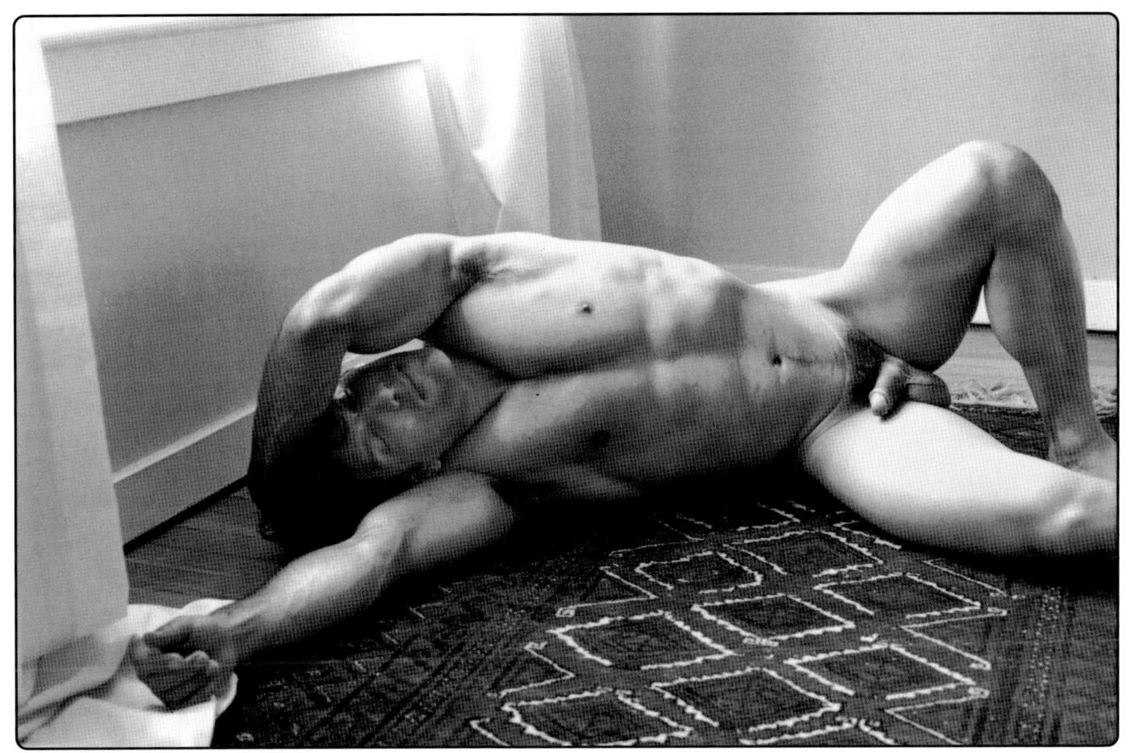

Marco   1990

totems of desire

photos by

Fehl Cannon

introduced by
José Villarrubia

éditions aubrey walter

DREAMERS

Fehl Cannon's men exist only for pleasure. In a space between conscious-ness and unconsciousness, at the twilight of cognition, they stand with their eyes shut, in introspective stances. The air in their world is heavy, a little denser than the one we breathe. It makes all movements slow and deliberate, like those of space explorers or deep-sea divers. Protagonists of a dream in which finding oneself undressed appears to be perfectly natural no matter how incongruous the context, they are not embarrassed by their nudity. On the contrary they seem to enjoy it, and liberated from their clothing, they become symbols, or totems of masculinity. The individual identities of the models in these images become lost, since Cannon turns them into players in a larger reverie. They are now cast in the roles of "the youth" or "the man" from the Classic standards of Greco-Roman beauty. These men explore their own bodies in their quotid-ian environments, and sometimes outdoors (mostly in nature). They languidly caress themselves, concentrating in erotic areas, which are often decorated with fetishistic paraphernalia. They are in an erotic dream, so they make love to each other, and since this is an all-male universe, homoerotic contact is the only possible form of intimacy.

There is little motion in these visions, for the models sit still, in traditional poses for the camera. The absence of color in these images unifies them, but the subjects belong to many races, and exhibit the beauty of youthful body types in different shapes and sizes. Illuminated primarily by natural light, their smooth, soft skin appears inviting, presented for our erotic inspection some-times totally bare and others bound in a variety of materials. This interest in bondage points to one of the underlying themes in these images: the struggle for power, for controlling and being controlled, implicit in all sexuality. But Can-non carefully avoids making his images jarring or violent. These photographs are done in the spirit of those from the early Twentieth Century, when there was a certain naiveté and curiosity in discovering the nude body photographically. Those candid shots eventually gave way to more elaborate and explicit sexual images, as photographic pornography developed. But in Cannon's case that transition never occurred.

There is a timeless quality to most of these photographs; the men could belong to any decade of the last century. This illusion is only altered in the instances when the models are adorned by contemporary body modification: piercings and tattoos, which draw our attention to their erogenous zones. The eternal pairing of pleasure and pain is implicit in these markings. In addition to their eyes being closed, sometimes they are blindfolded, denied of the knowledge of their environment and even more vulnerable to the aggressive gaze of the camera. This sensory deprivation turns the viewers into their masters, those in charge to which they are submitting. But these captive men never look pained or humiliated. Cannon carefully preserves their dignity, and presents his models, regardless of their bindings, seemingly in control of the scenario. The most overt expression of this power is when in some of the images the models flirt with the camera, establishing eye contact with the viewer. They always sport the inviting look of someone who is enjoying being desired. That's the one instance when they awake from their slumber, when their gaze disturbs the liquid surface of reality. Their seductive stares encourage us to become part of their world.

Cannon has sometimes entered this dream by photographing himself alone and with some of his models. The resulting photographs blend seamlessly with the others in his body of work. By doing that he has totally submerged himself into his own fantasy. And by collecting his best images in this book, he is giving us a chance to do the same.

José Villarrubia

Baltimore, 2001

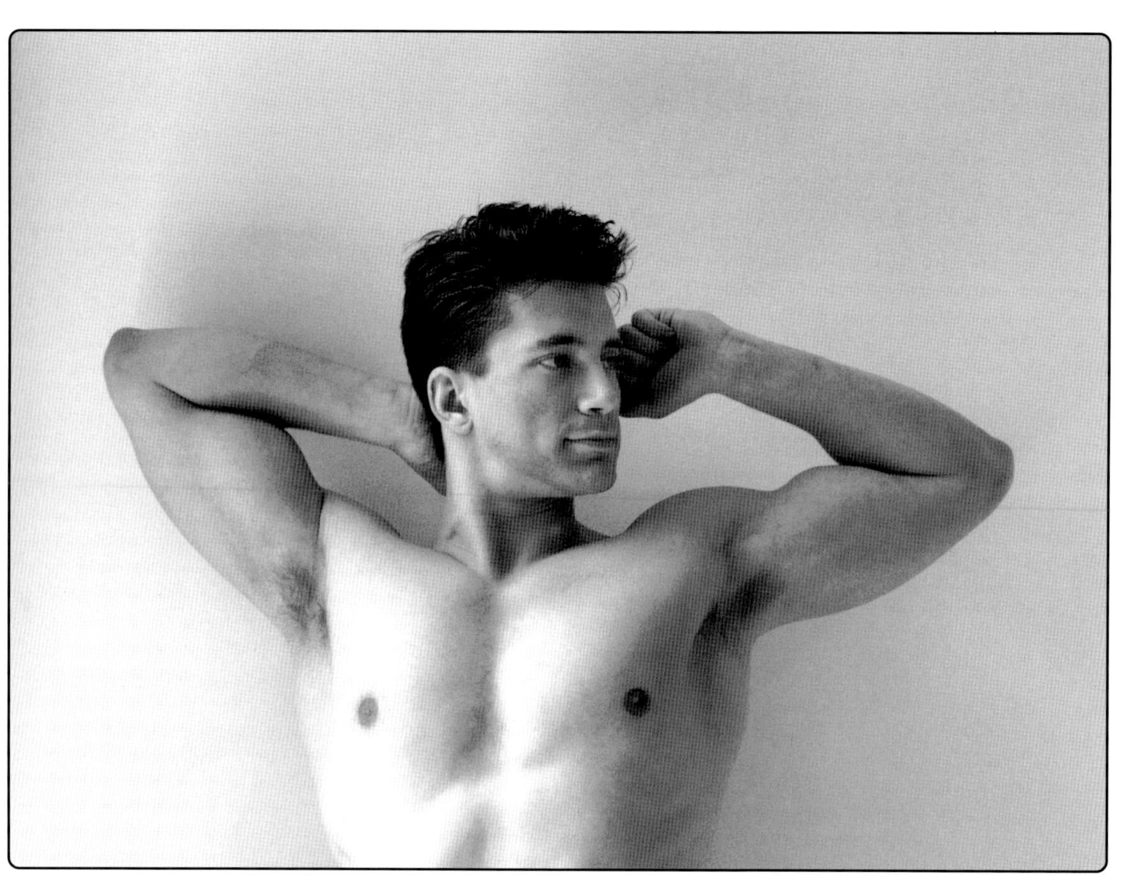

6   *José Antonio   1991*

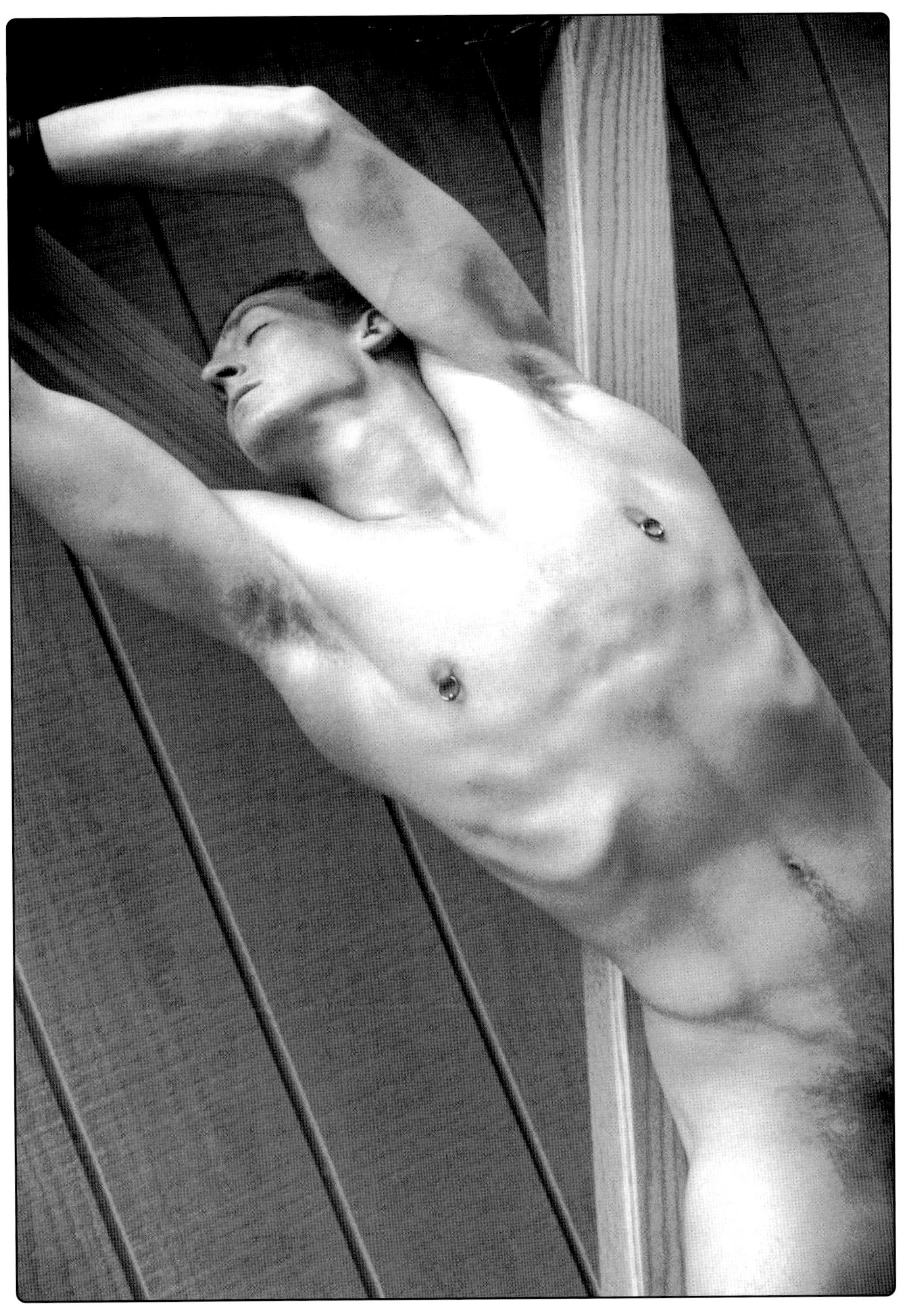

St. Andrew's Cross   2000

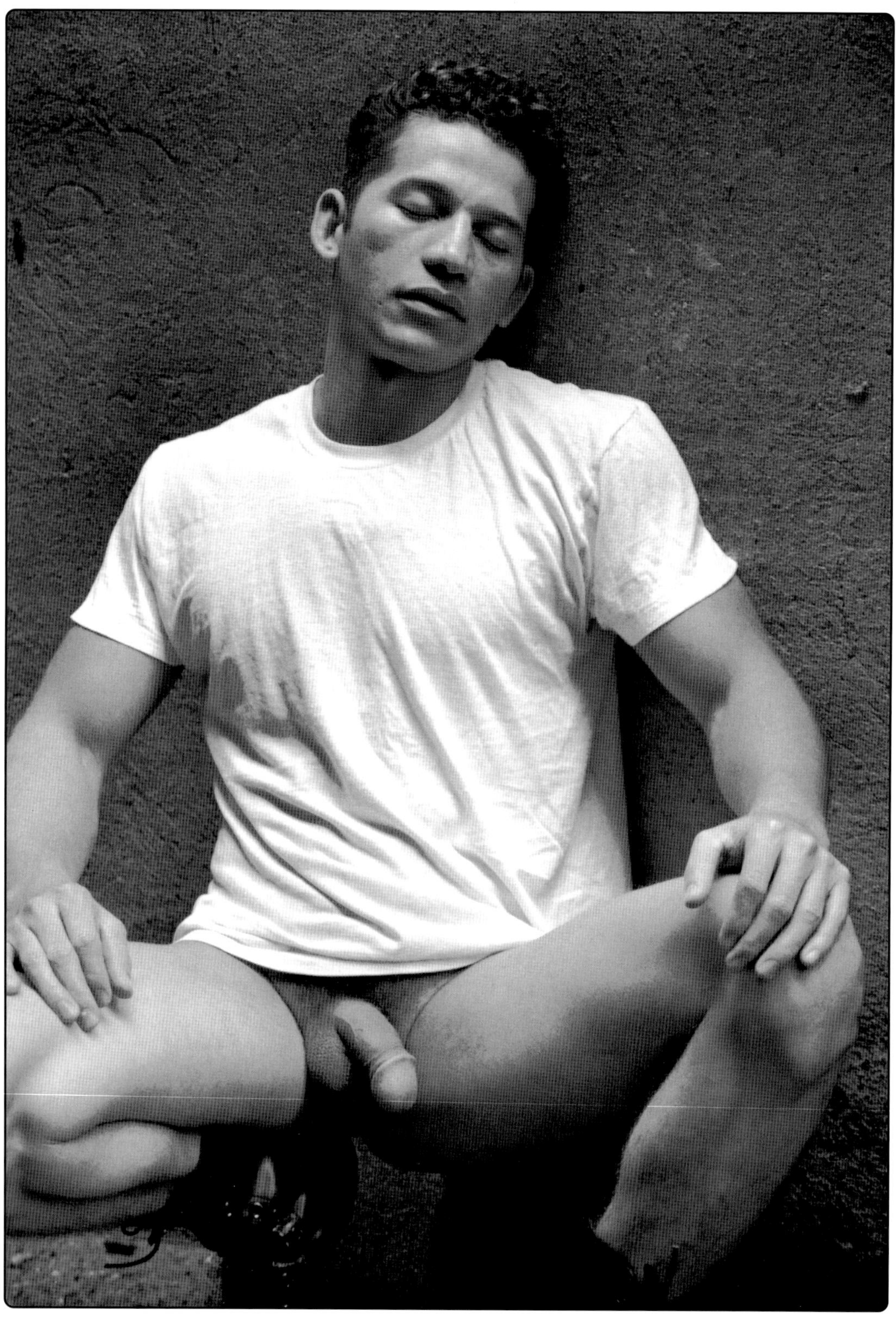

8   *White T   2000*

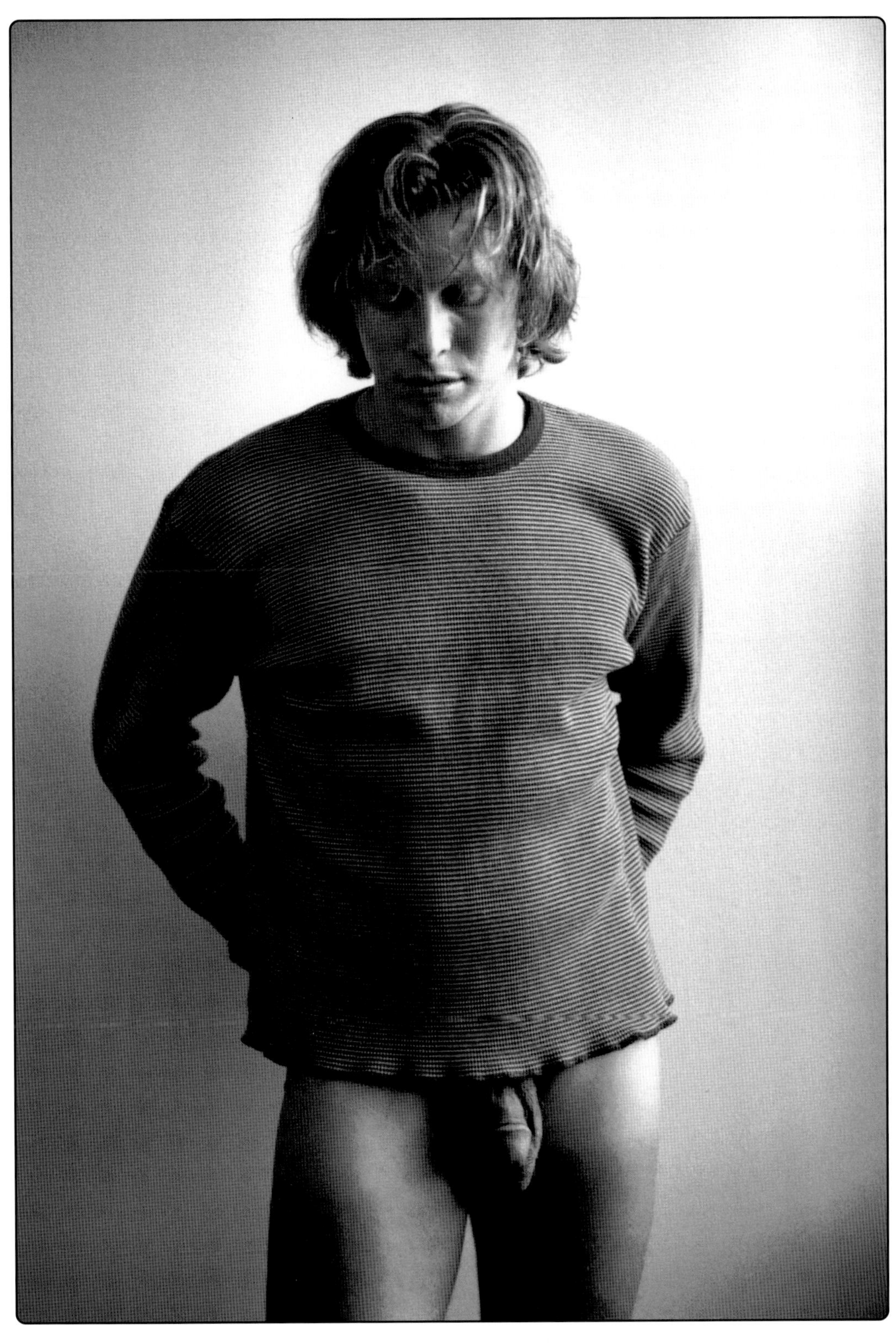

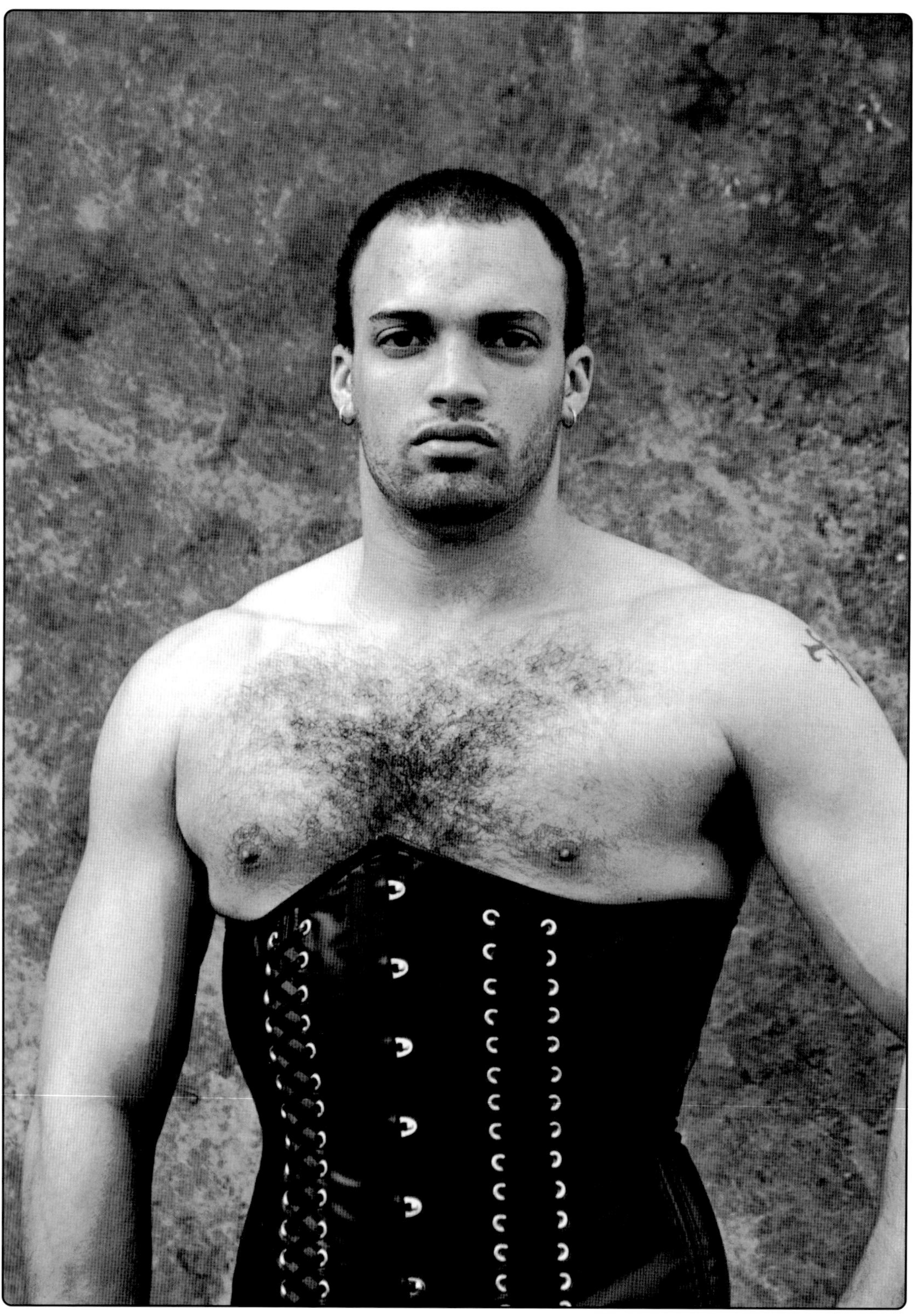

10   Kobe   1999

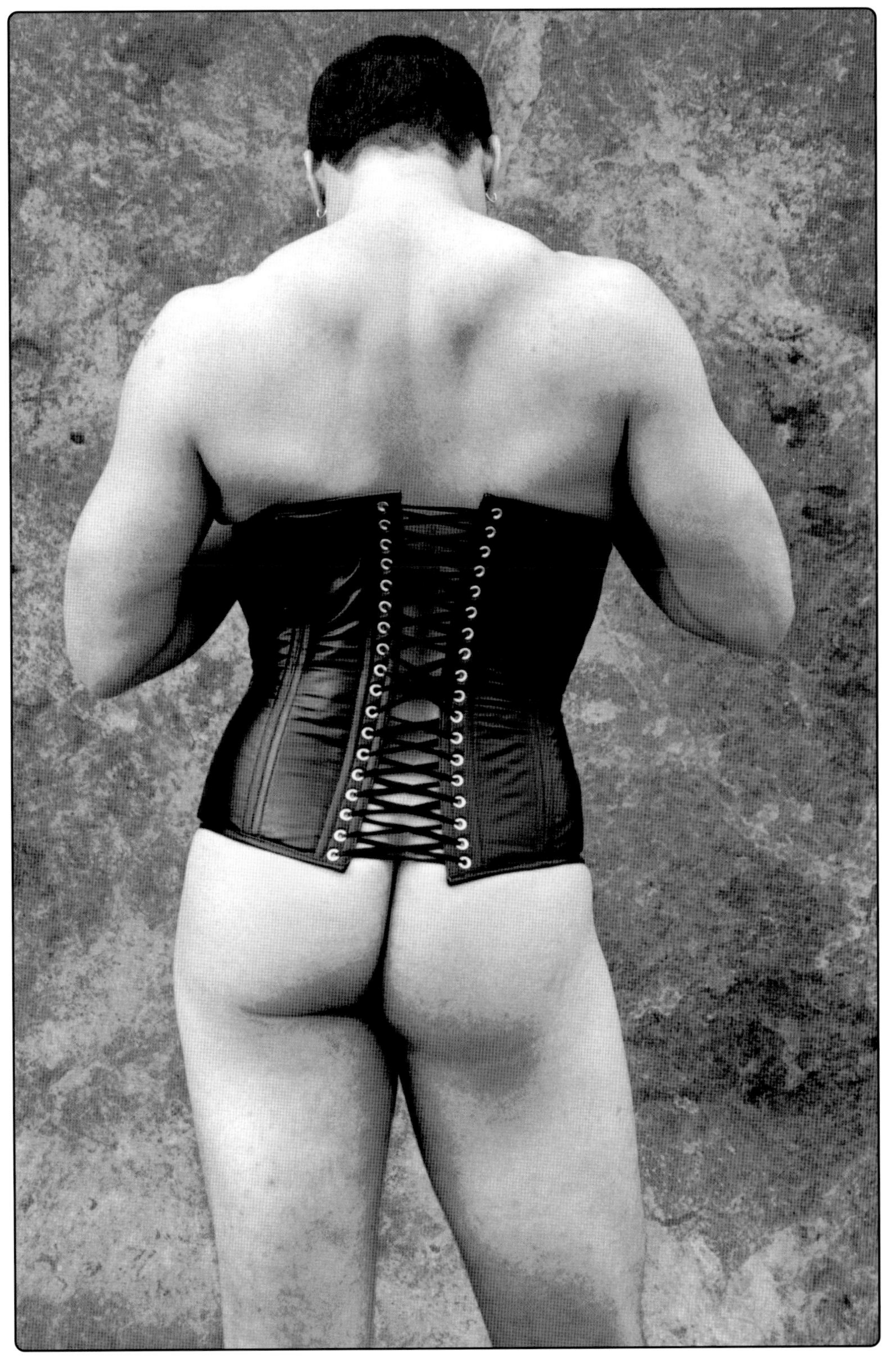

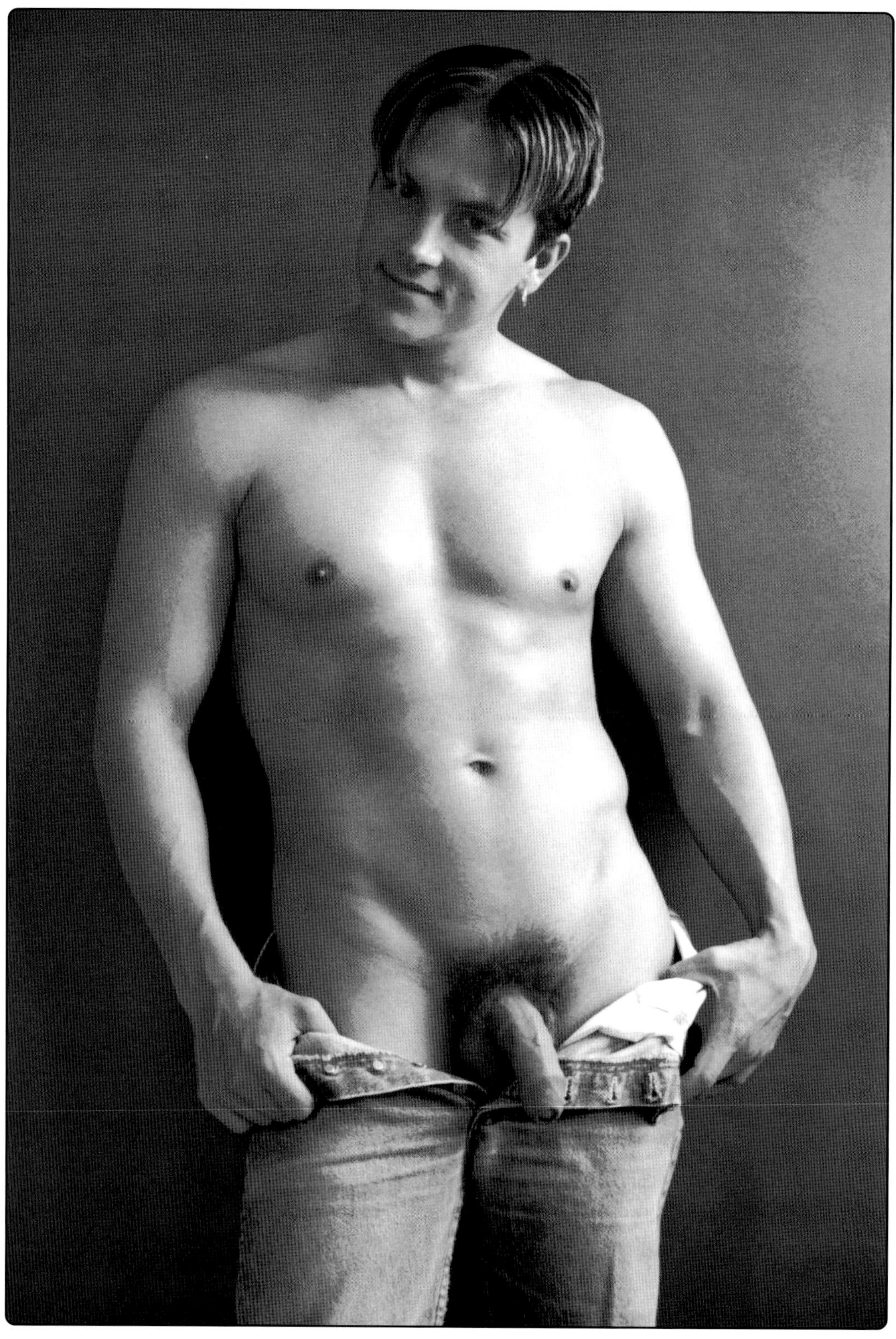

12   Denim   2000

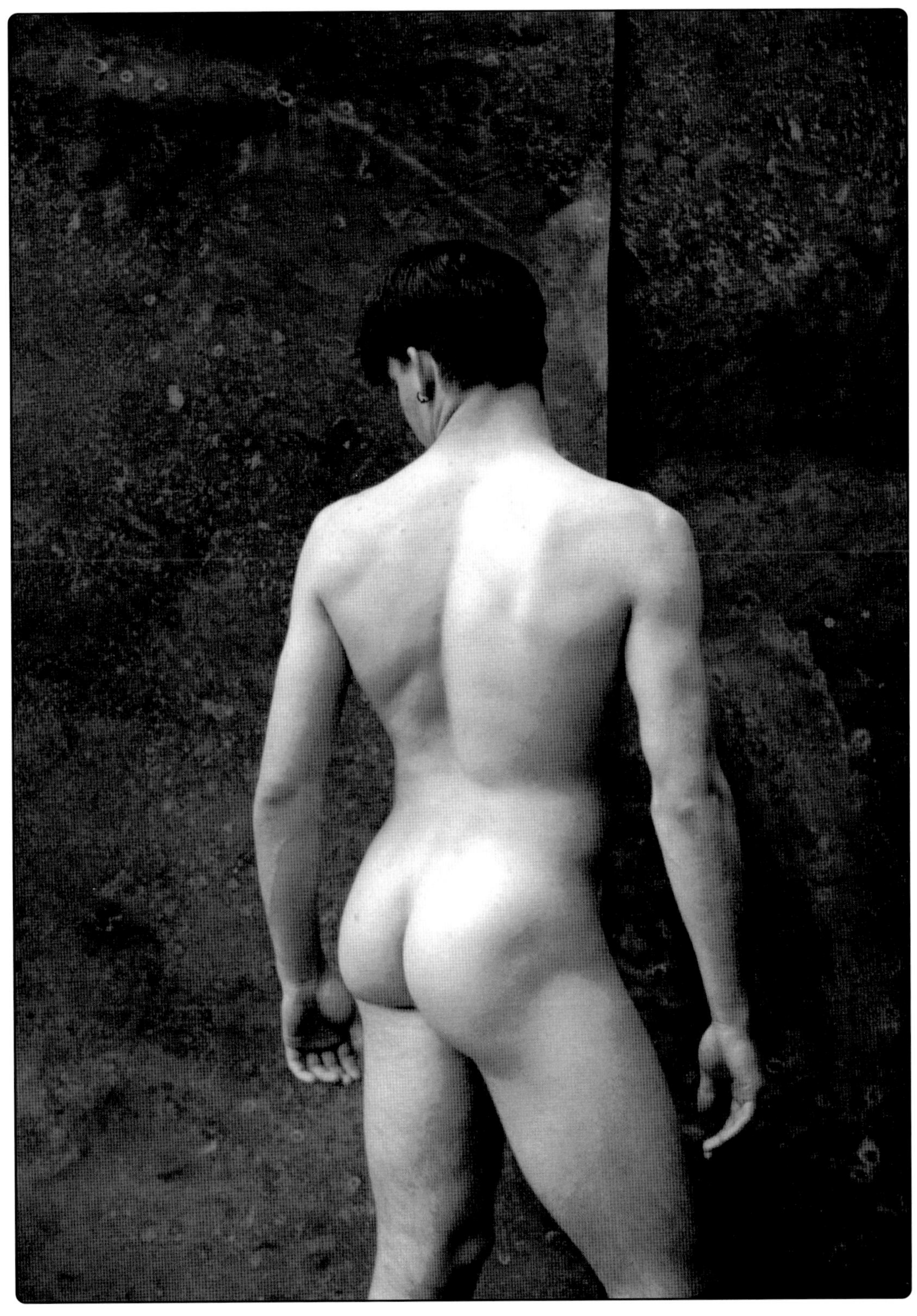

Back 1997 13

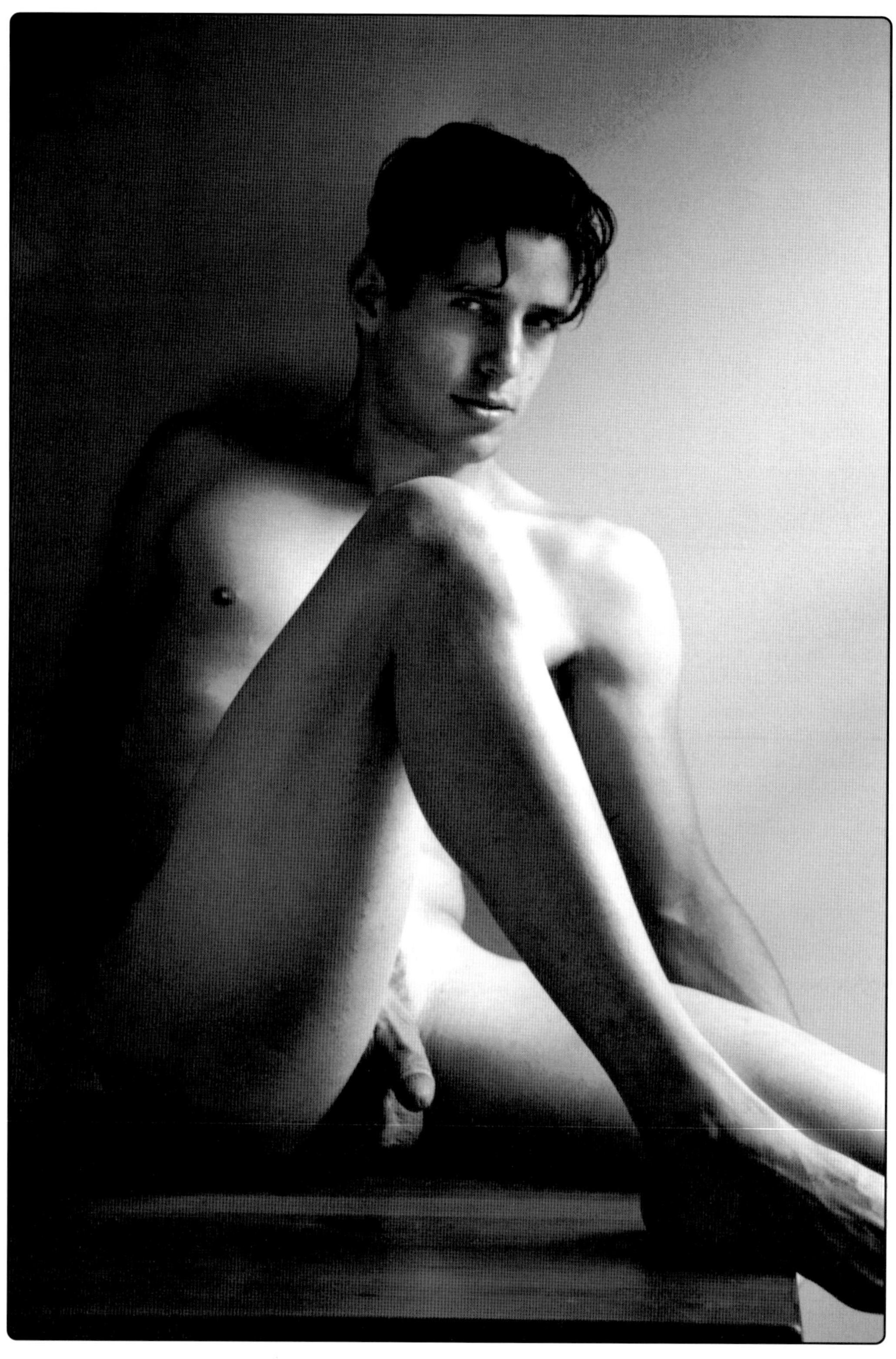

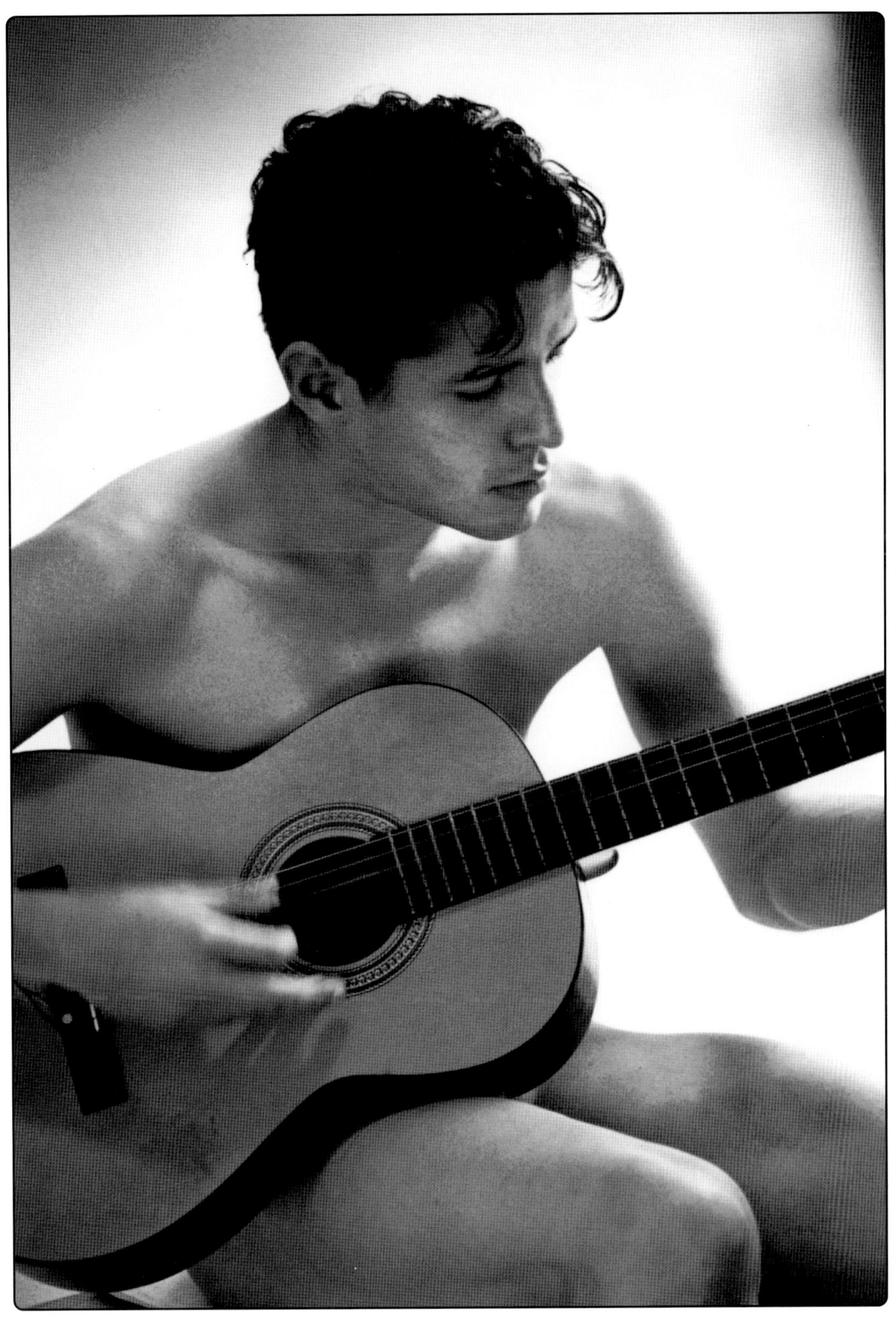

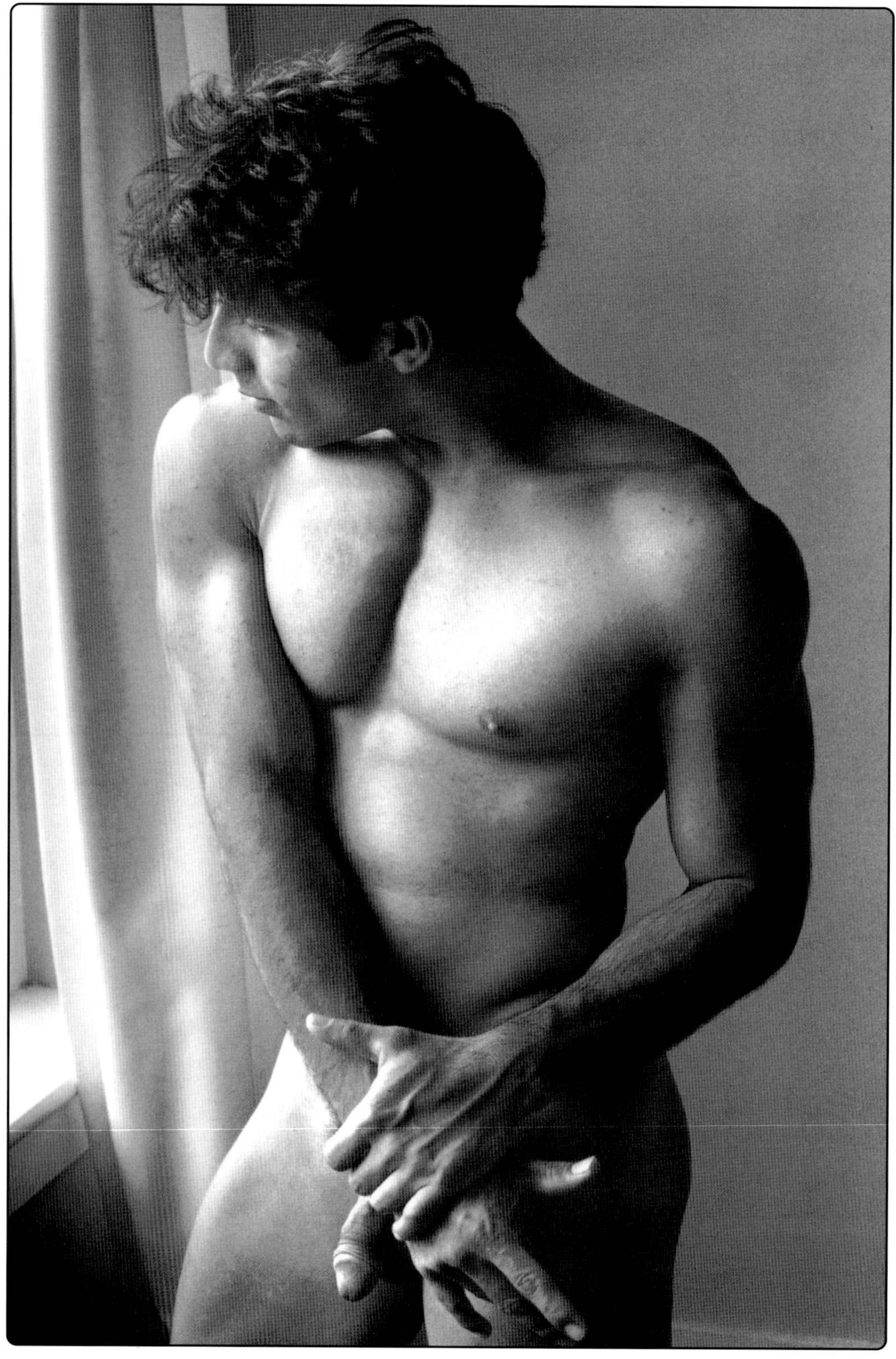

16   *After the Workout   1991*

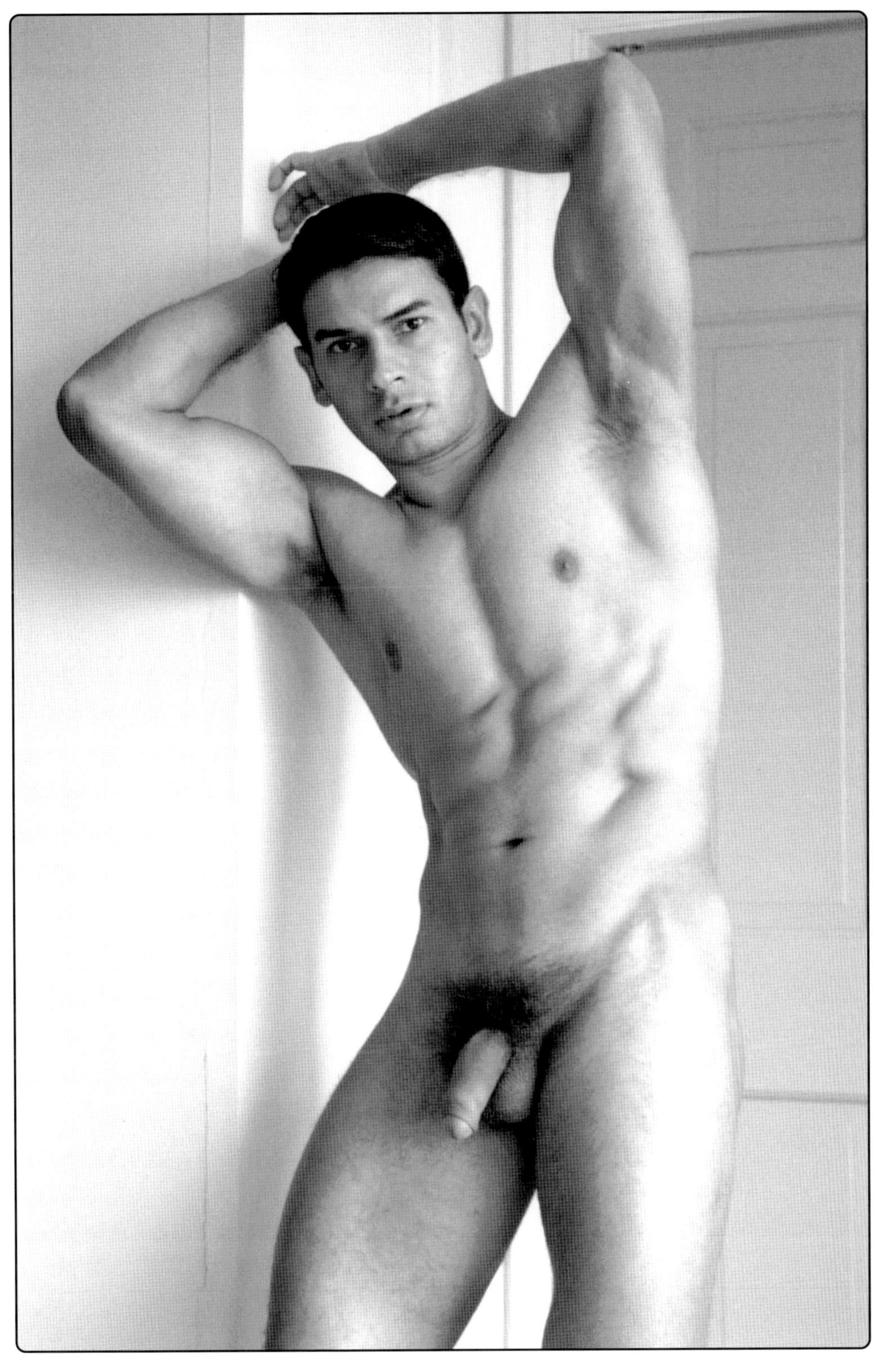

Gilberto   1998   17

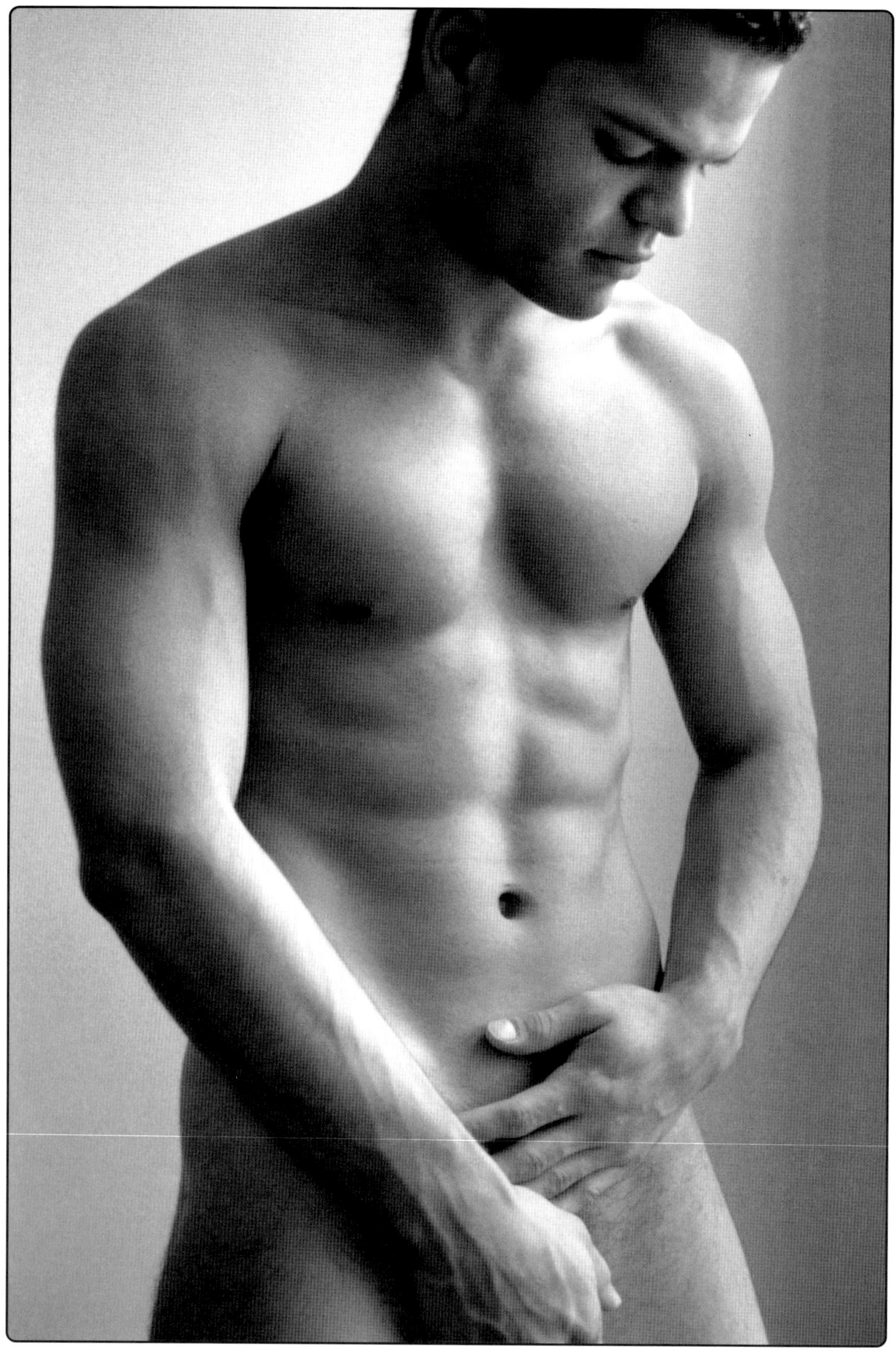

18   Hara   2000

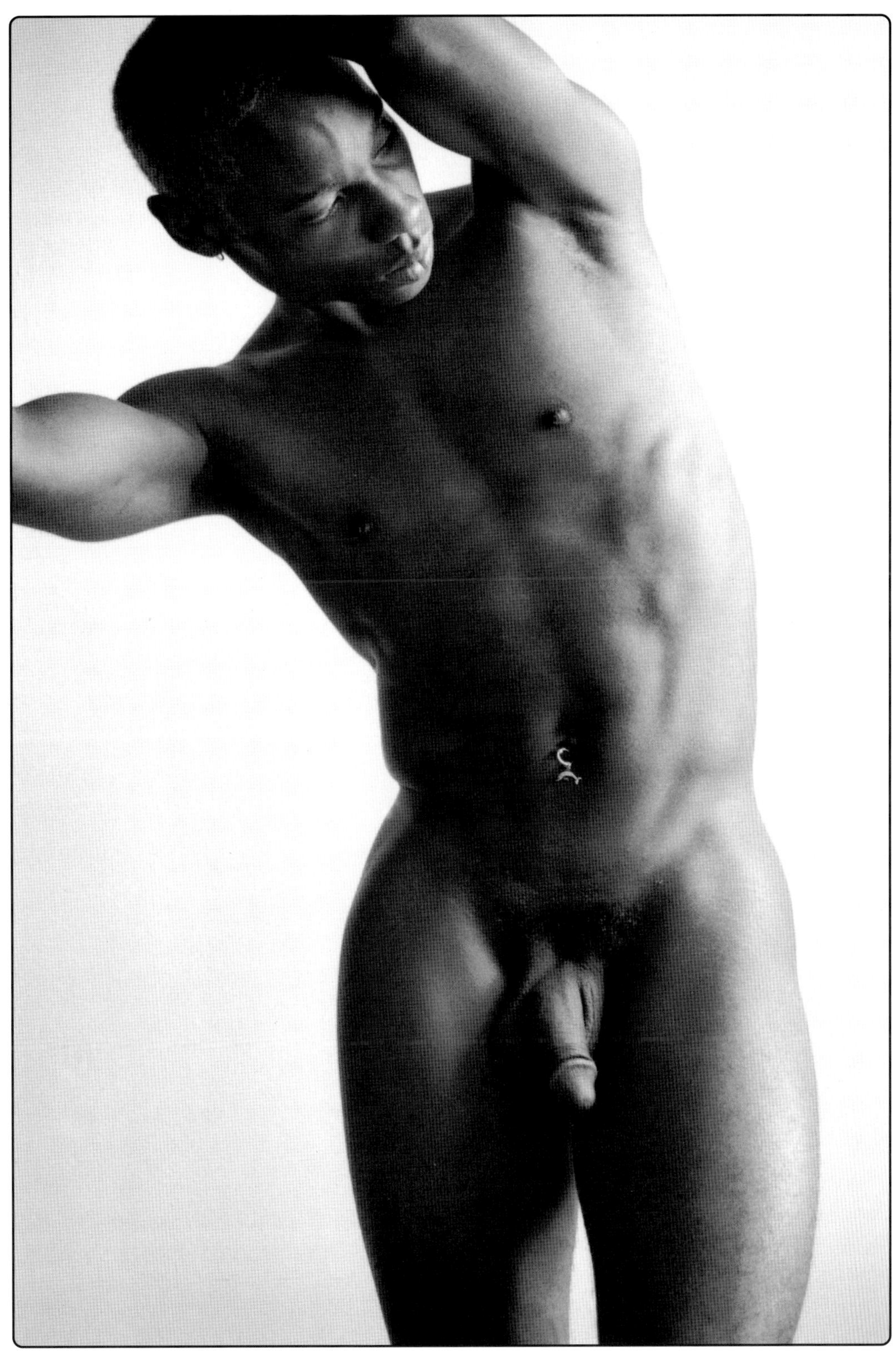

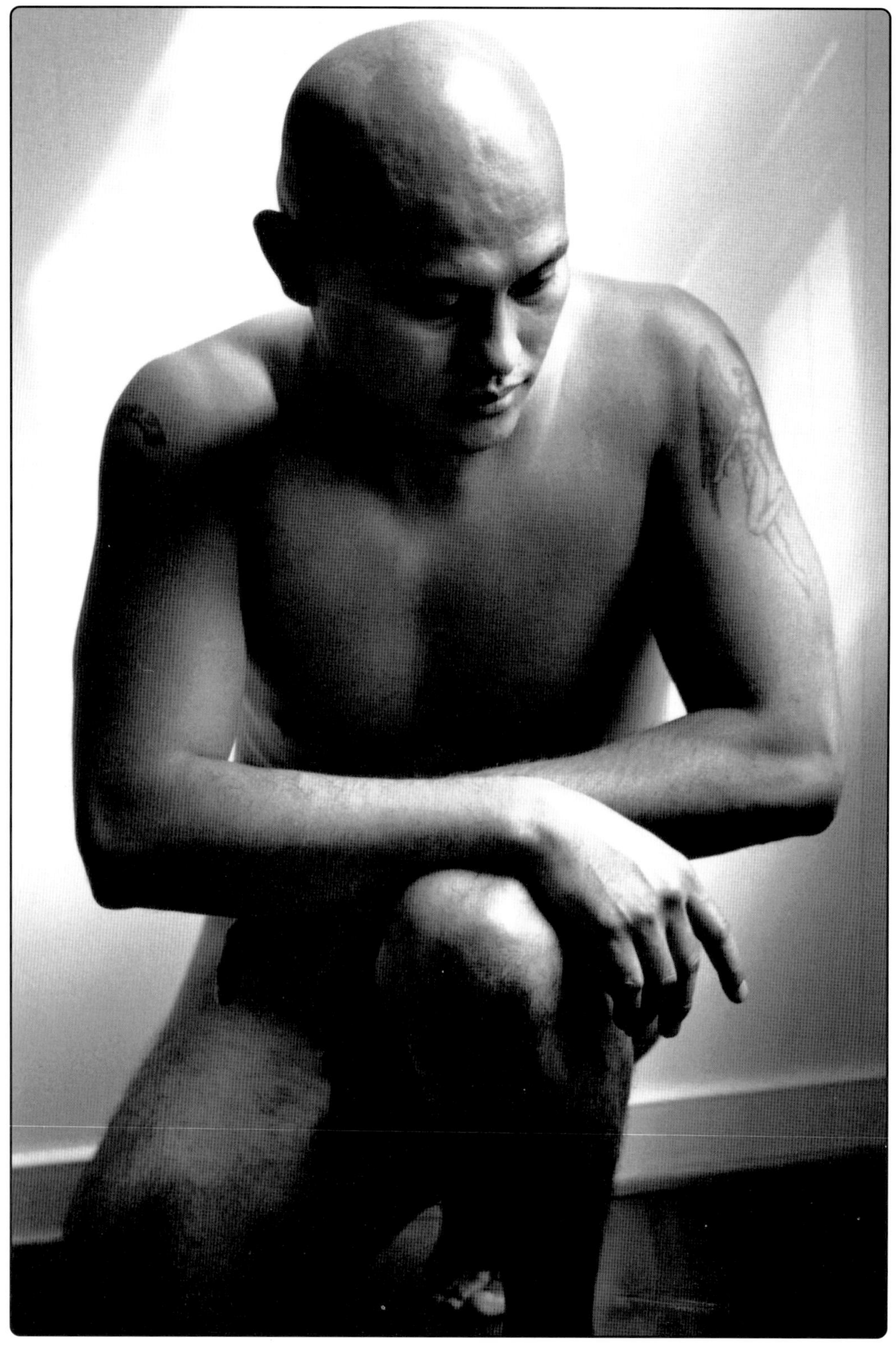

20   Angel   2000

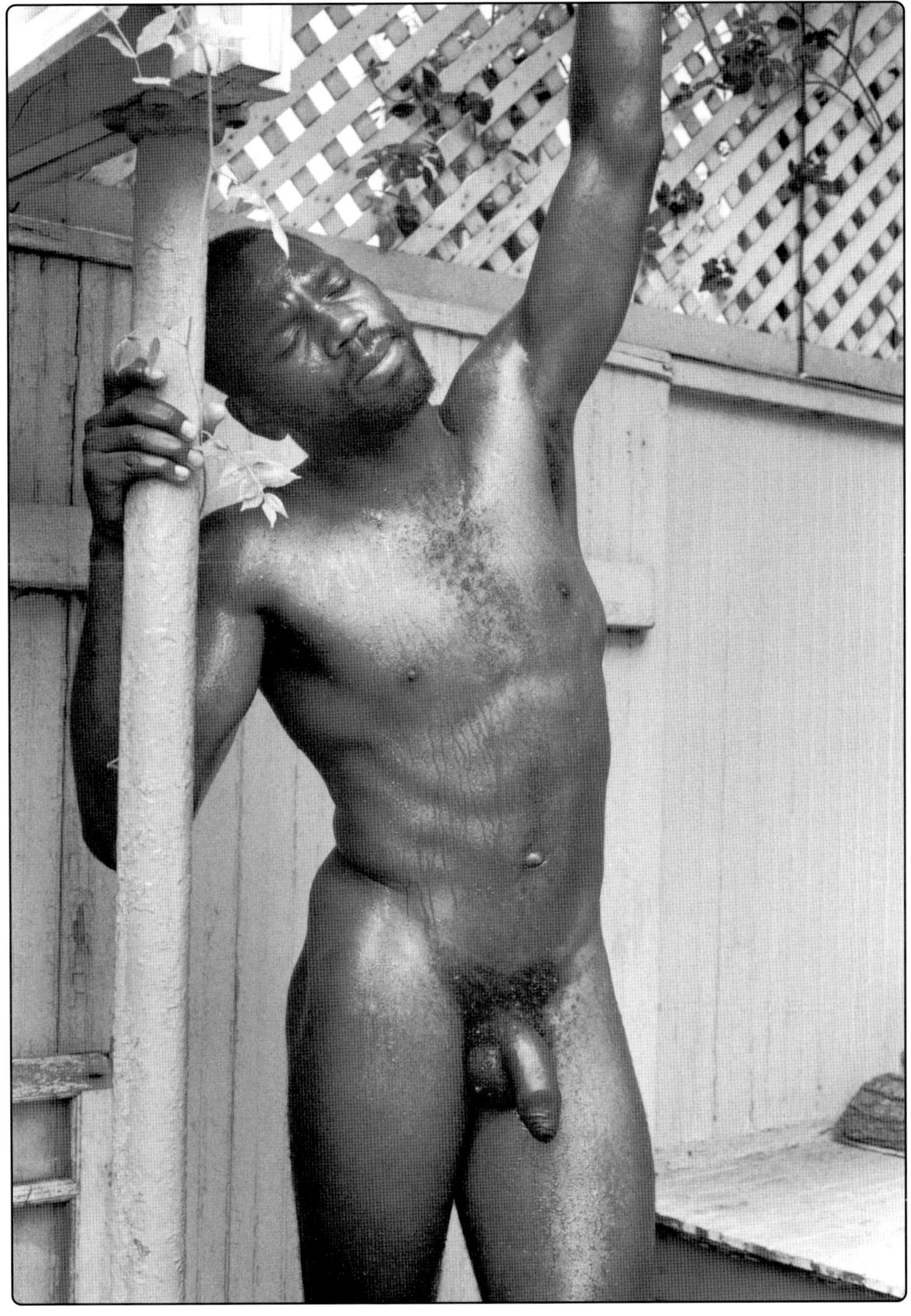

Anthony   1986   21

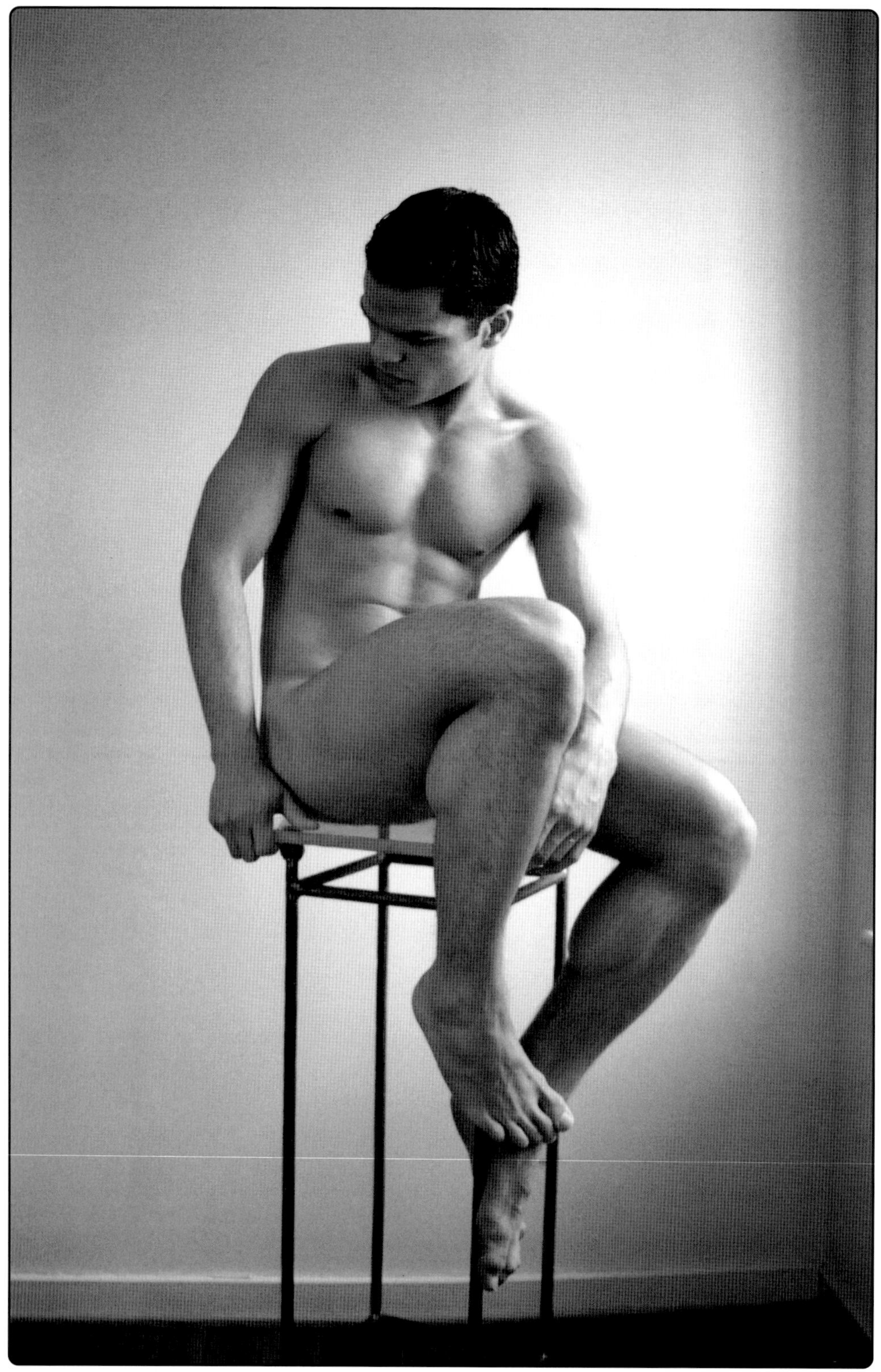

22   *Seated Nude   2000*

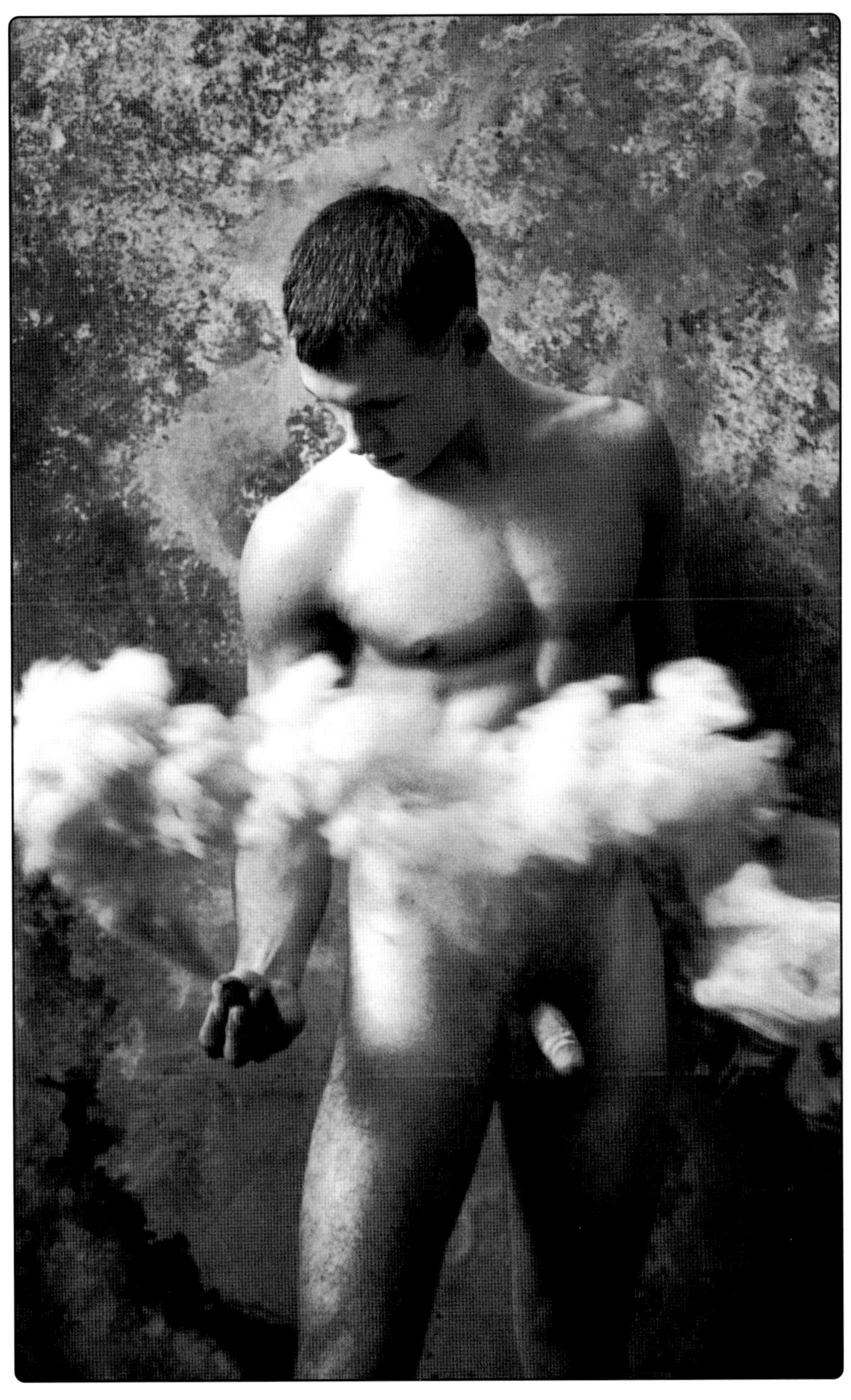

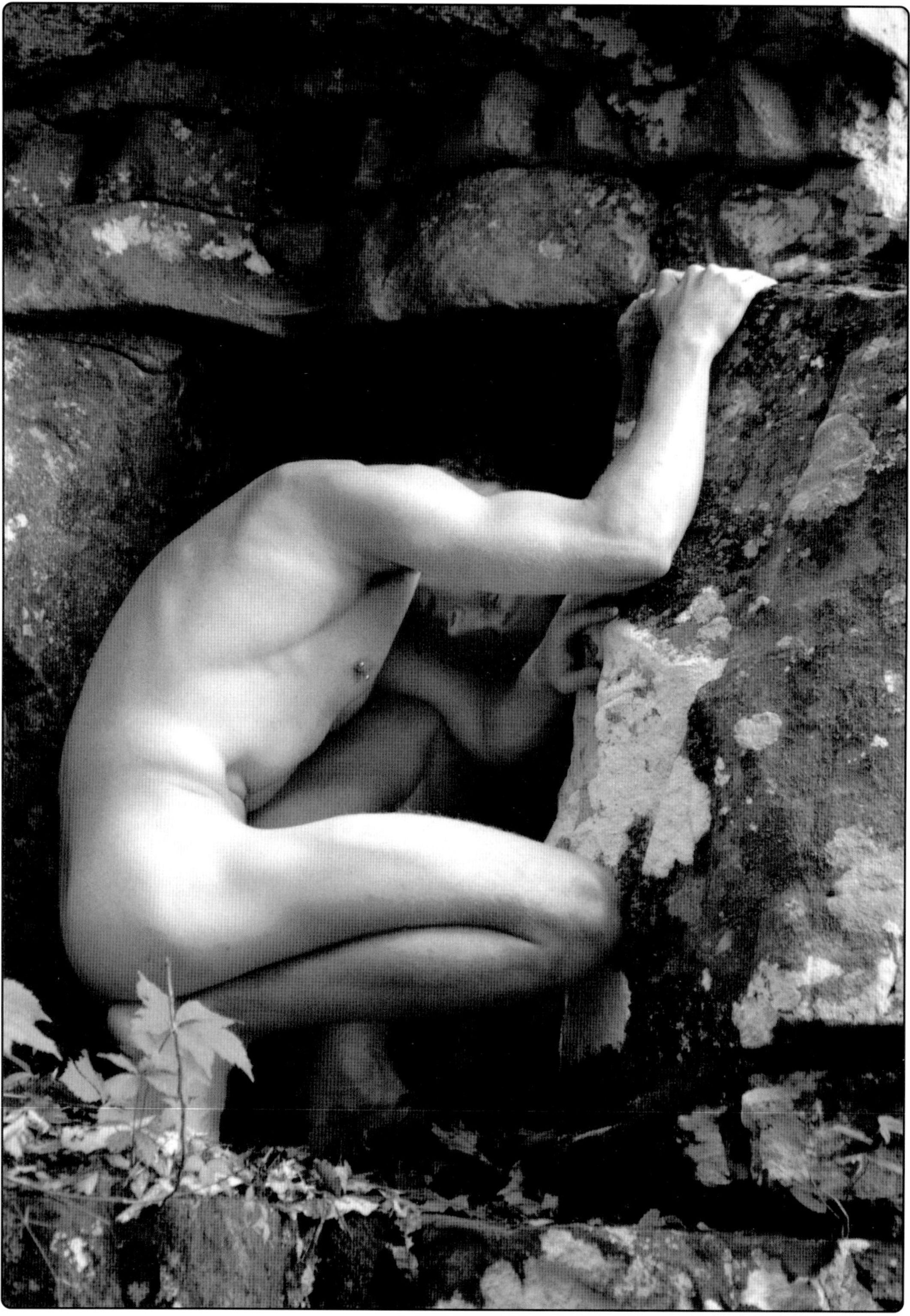

24   *Nude with Stones   1982*

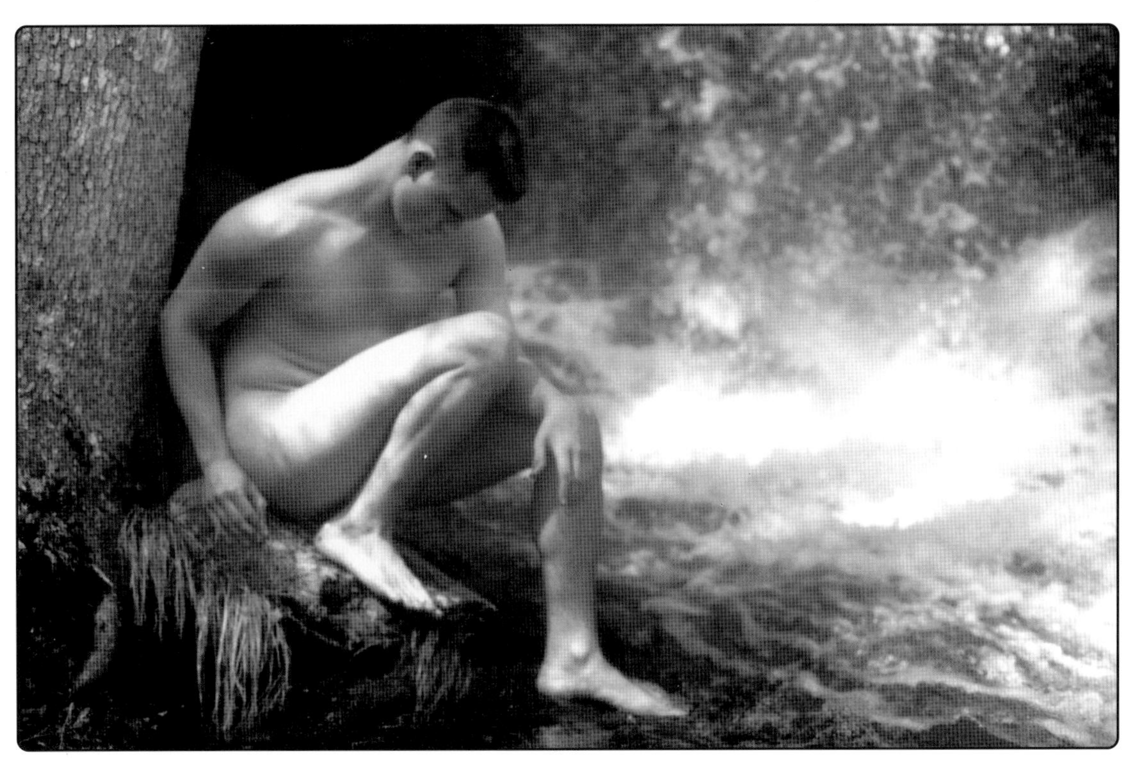

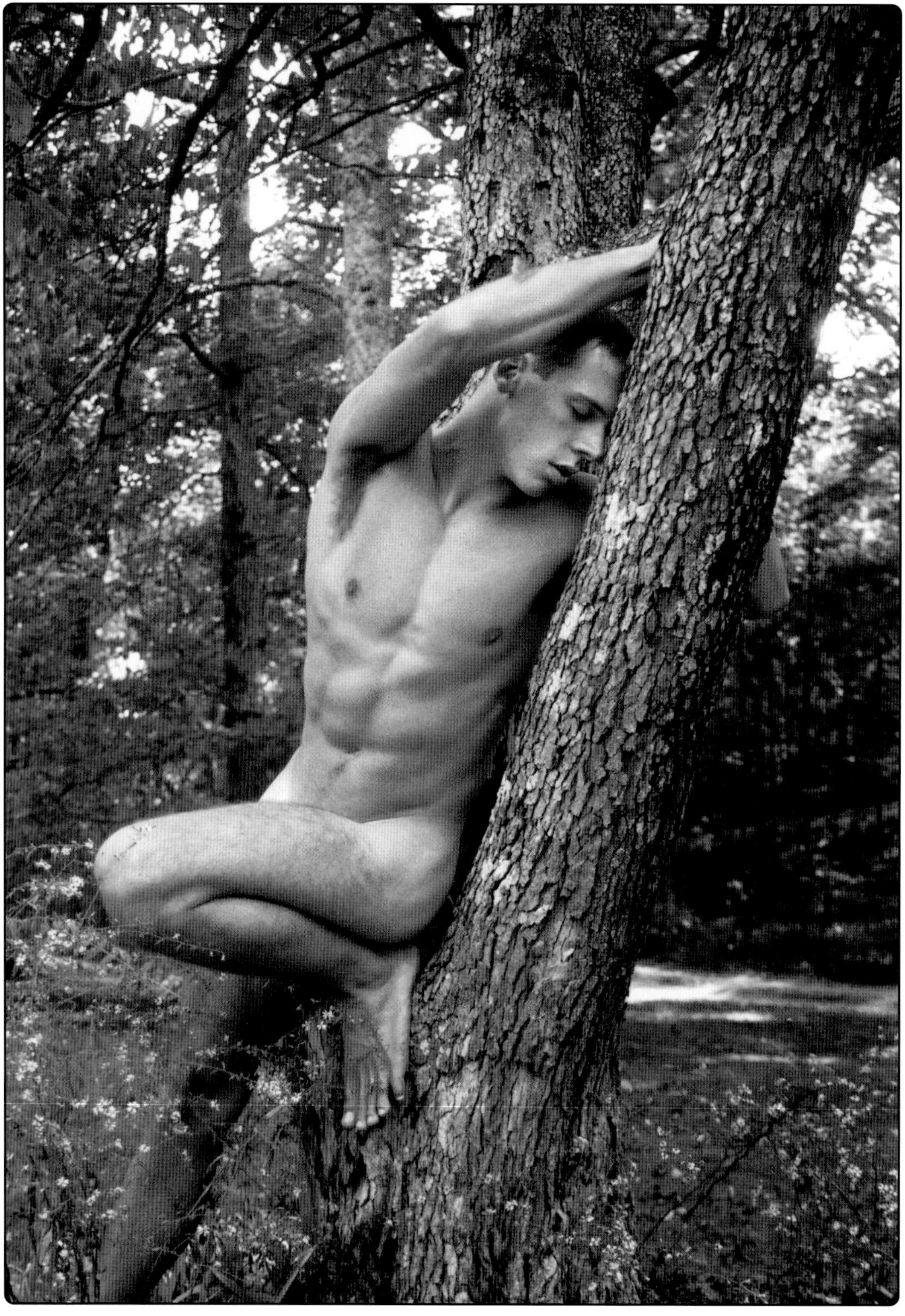

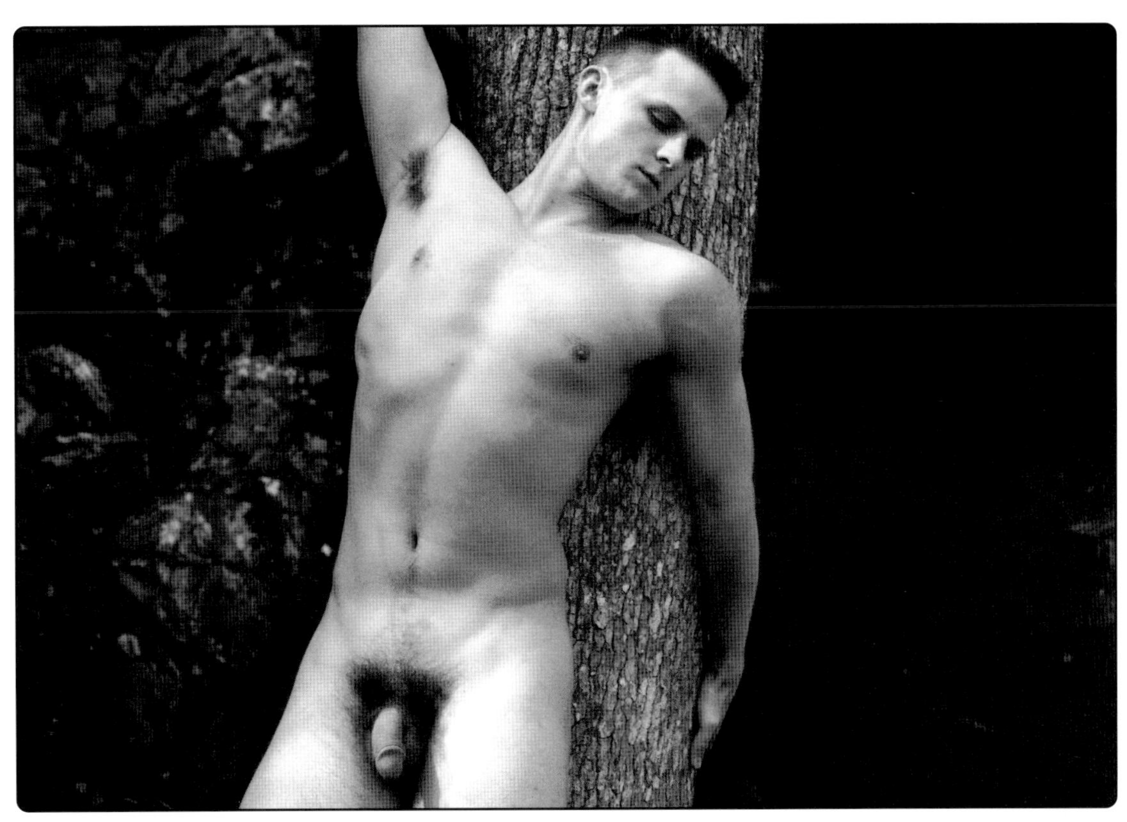

Sebastian   *1993*   *27*

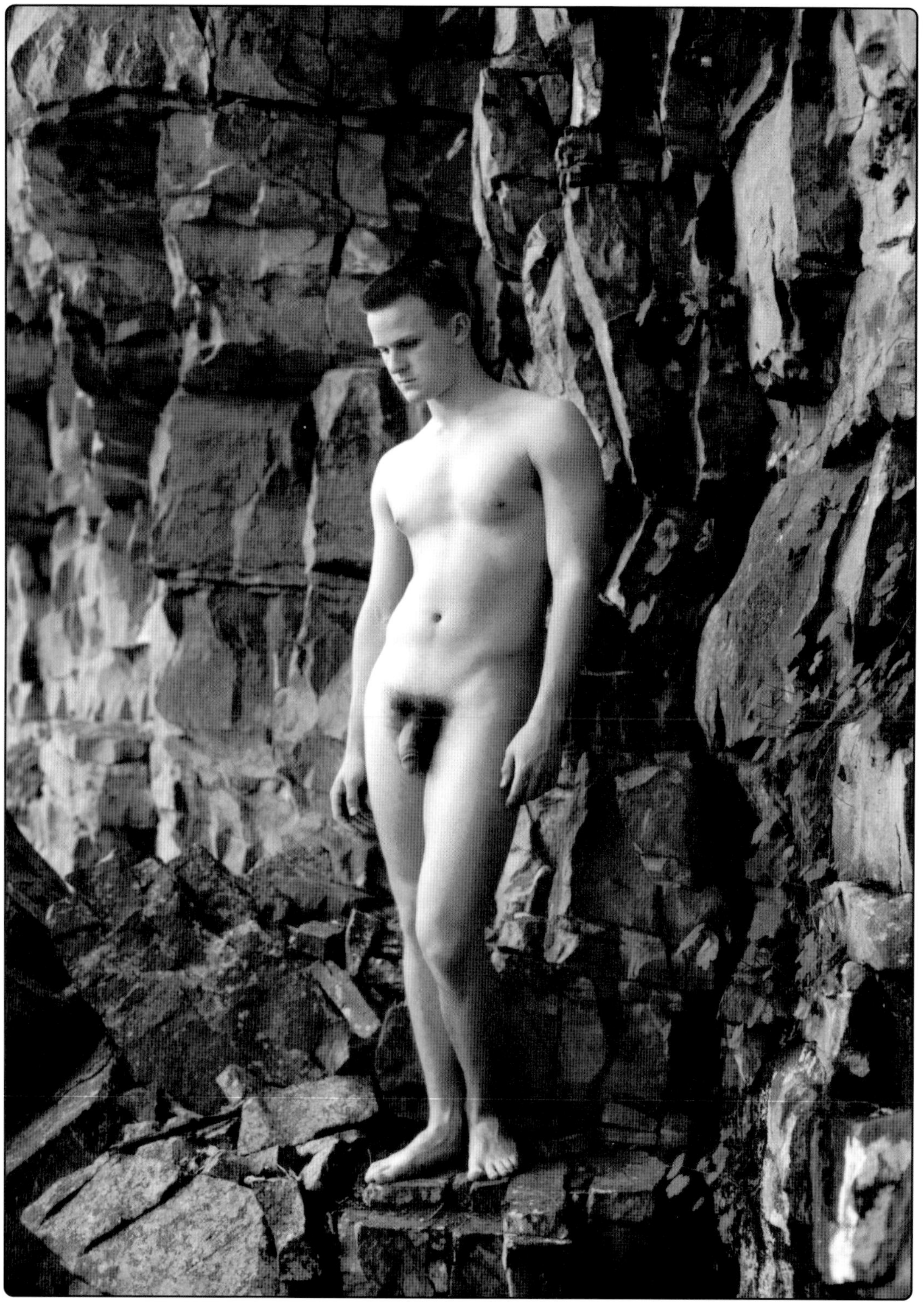

28   *Exile   1993*

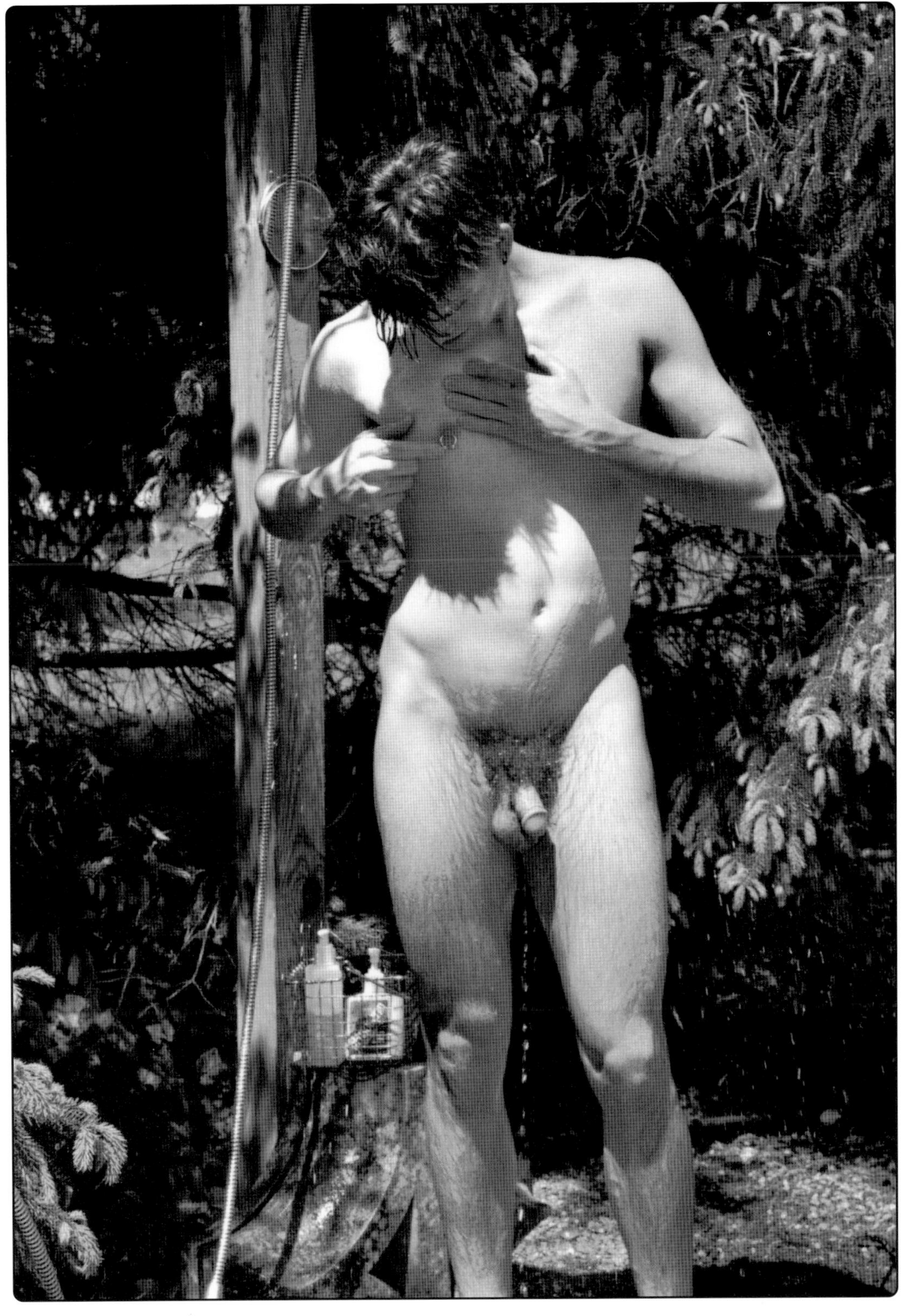

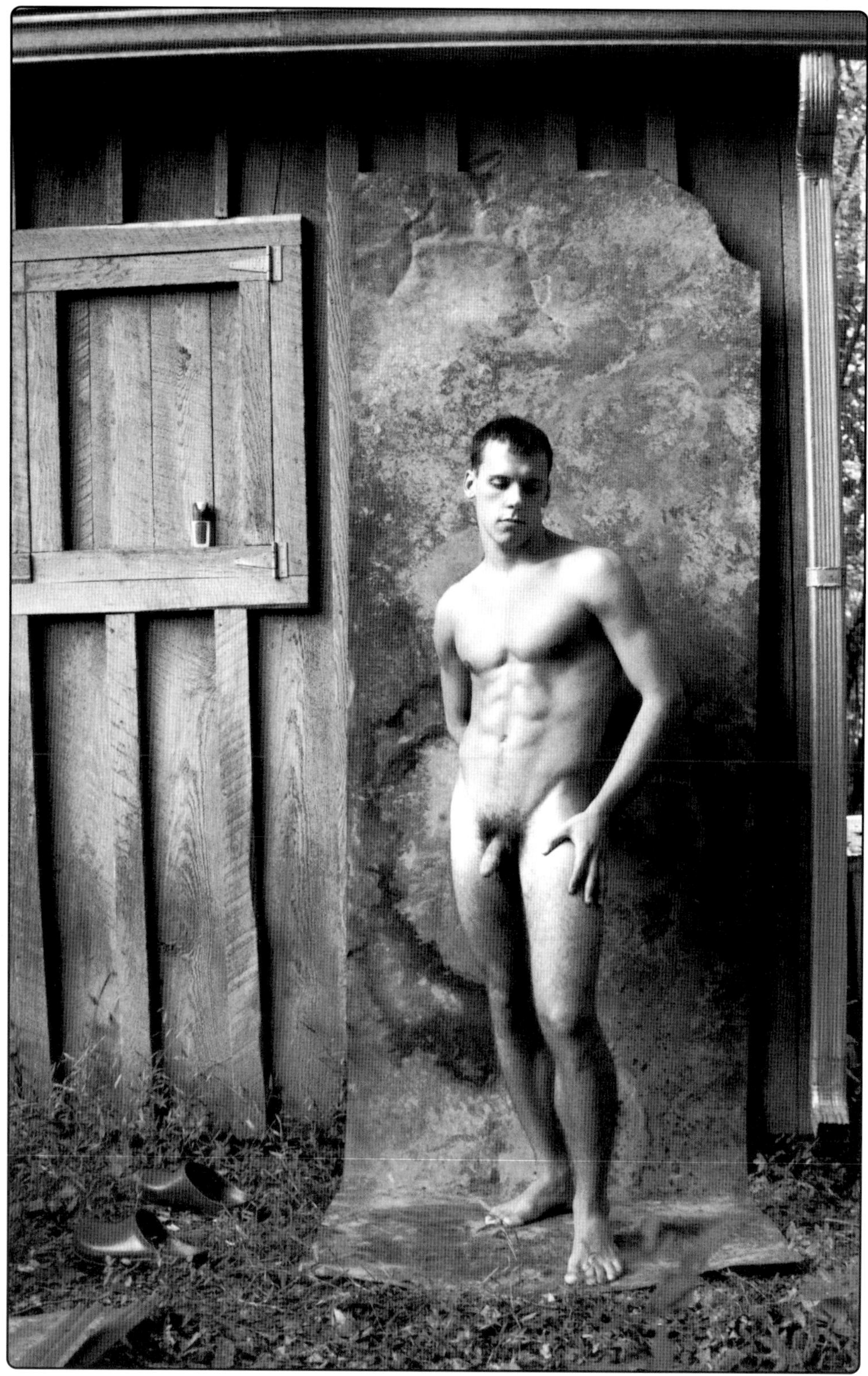

    The Photo Shoot   2000

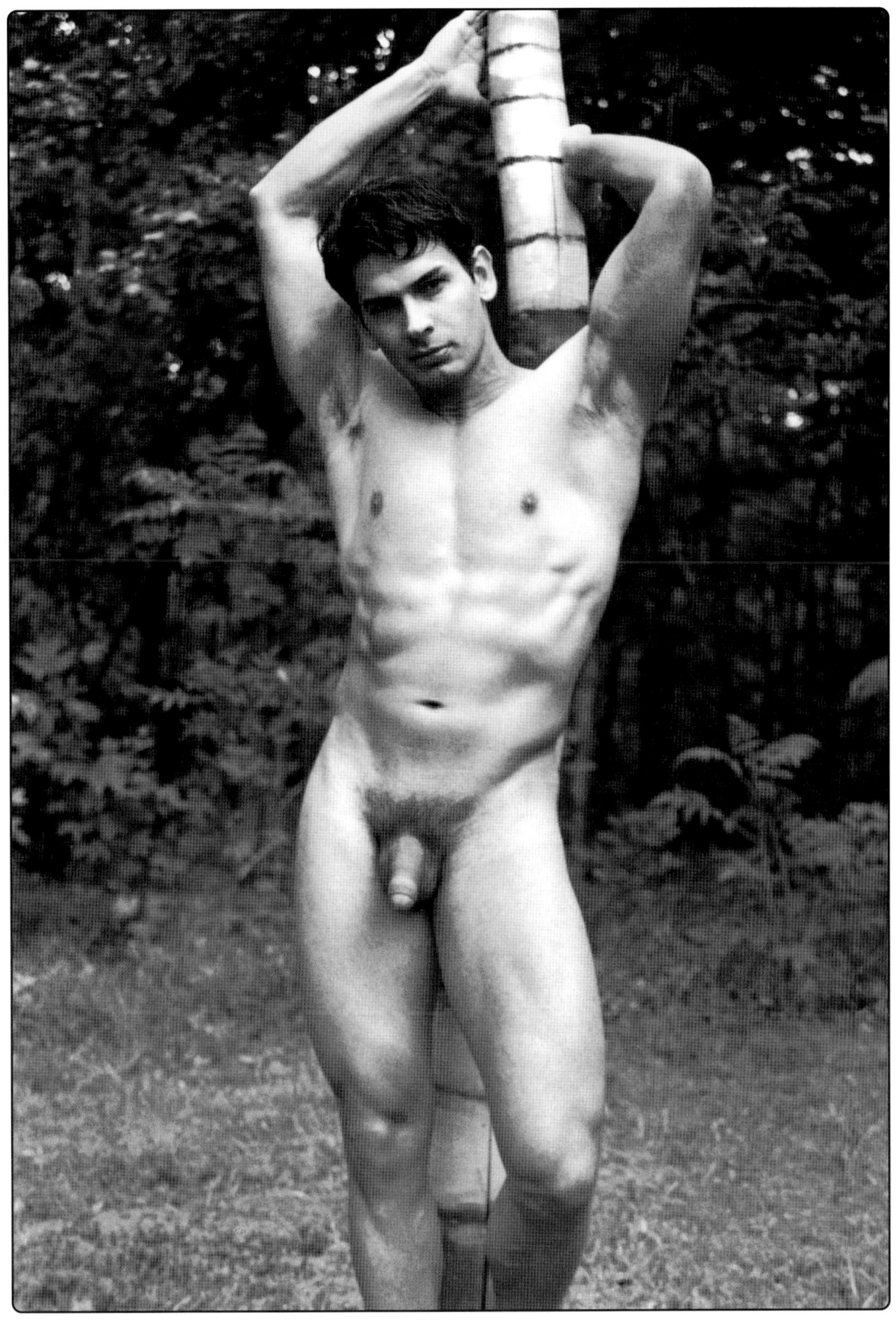

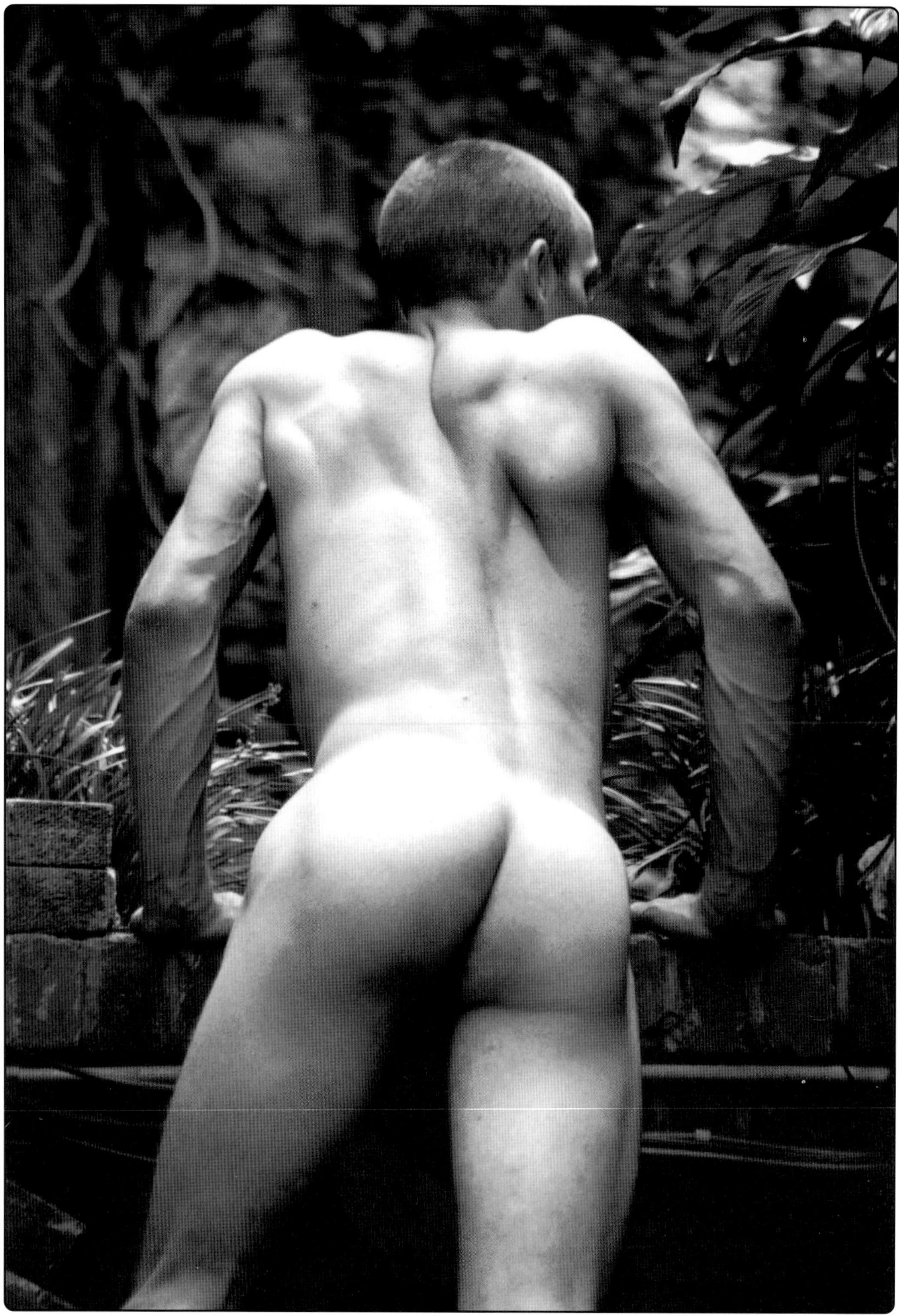

32   *Garden Wall*   *2000*

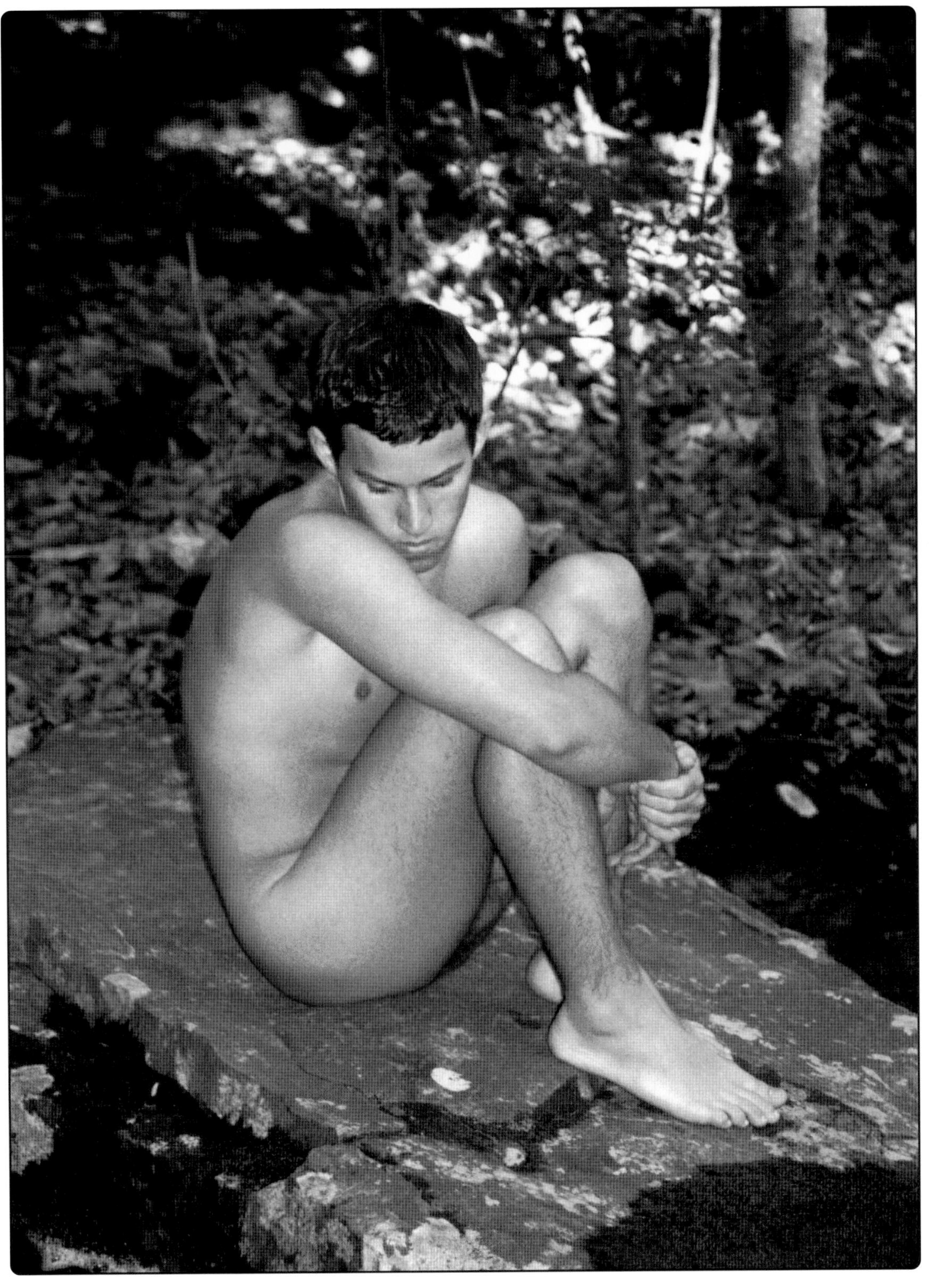

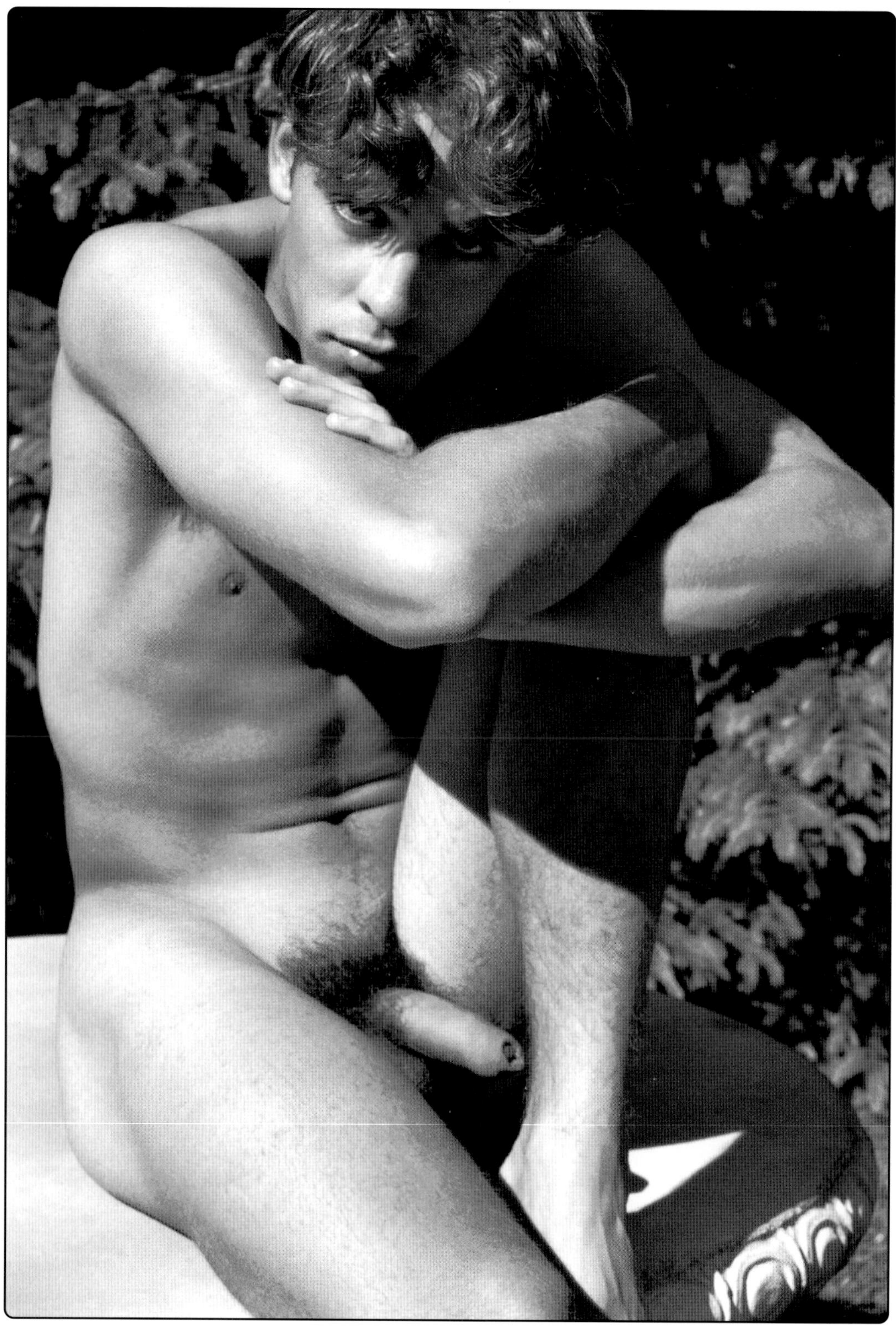

34   Billy   1997

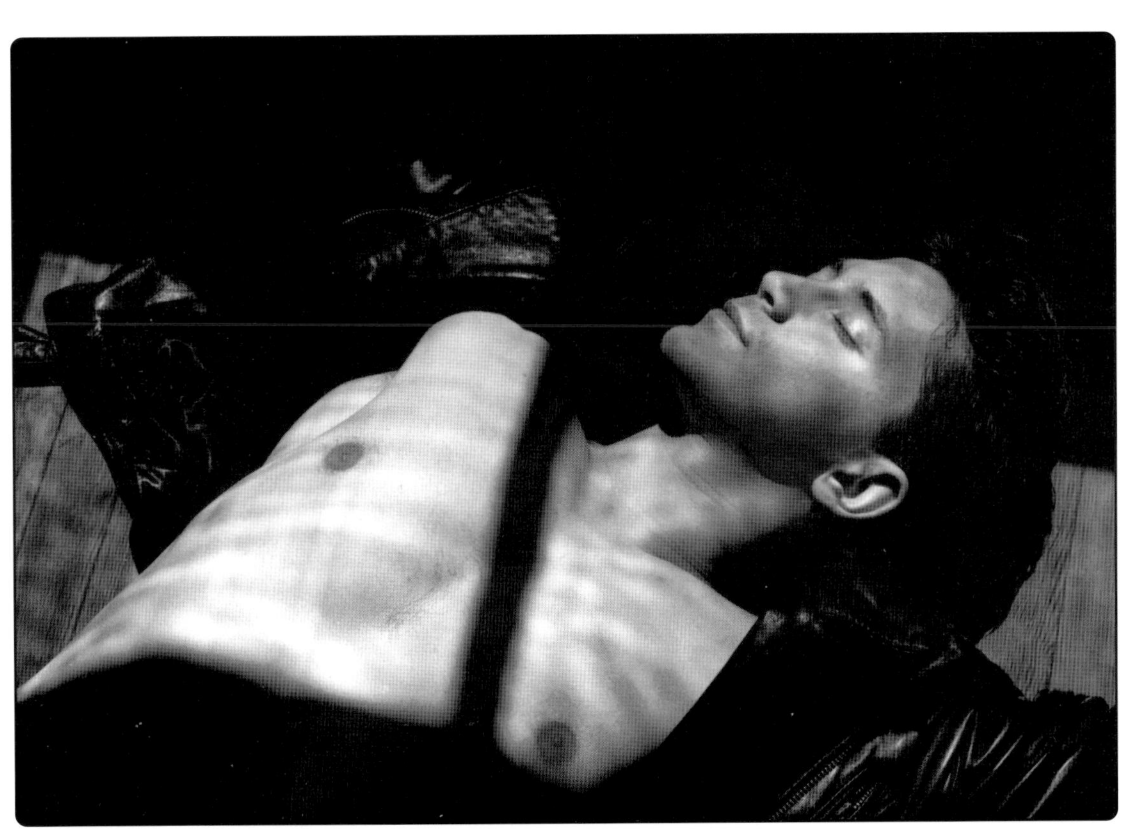

Leather Jacket Dream   *1991*

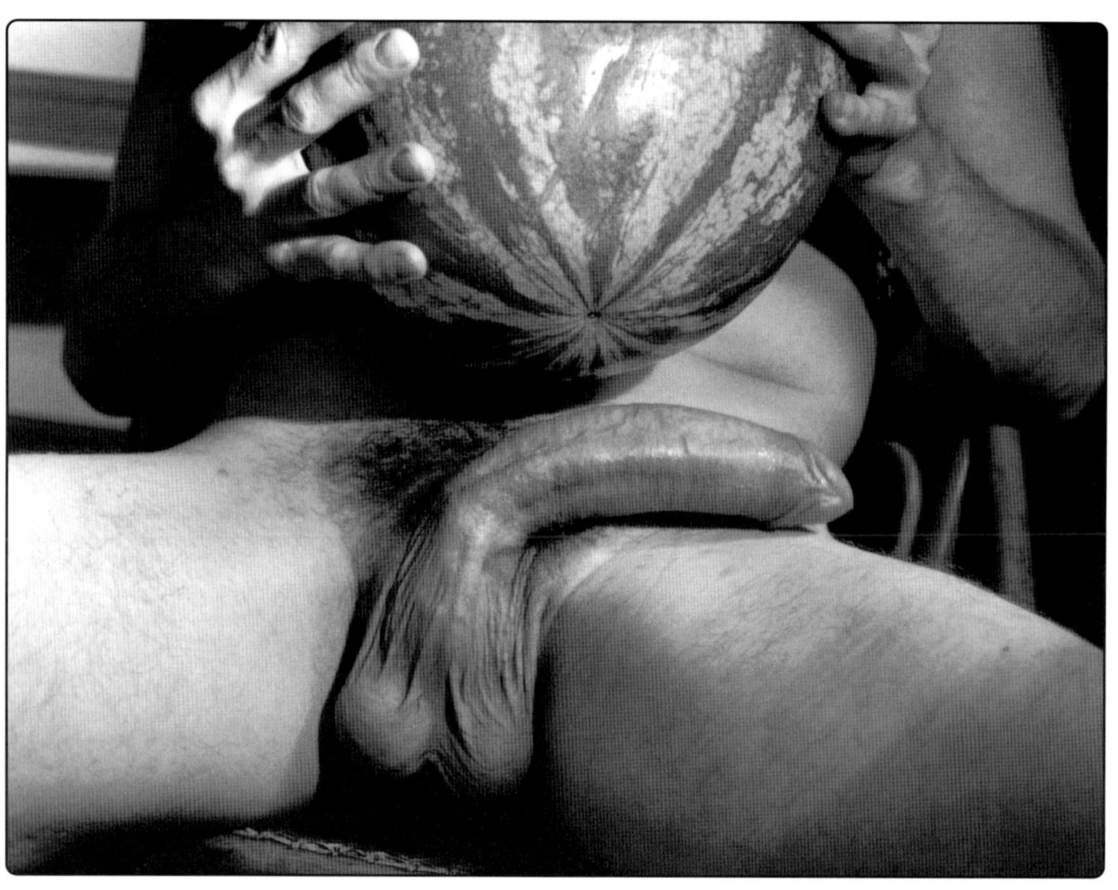

36   *Watermelon*   *1997*

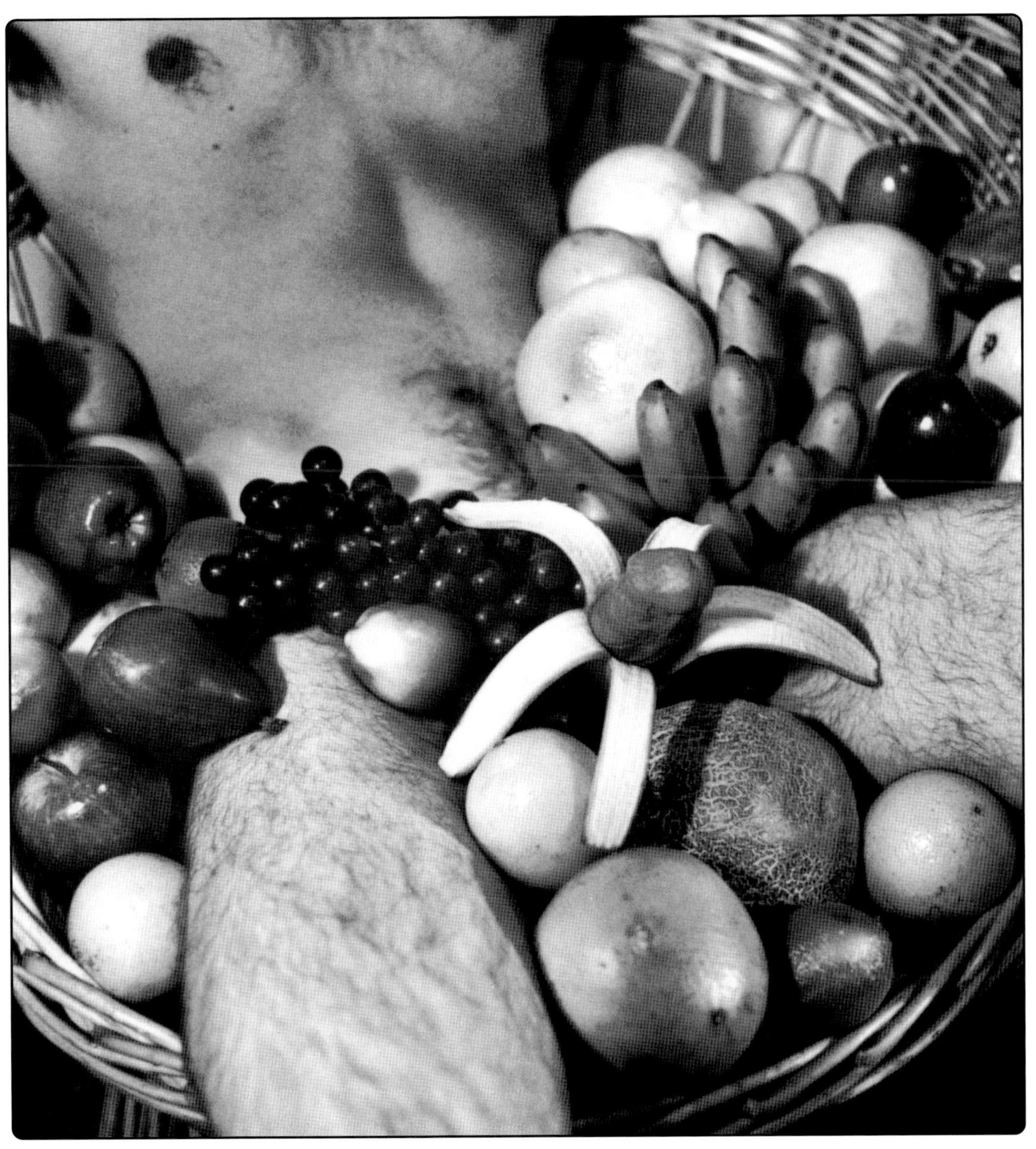

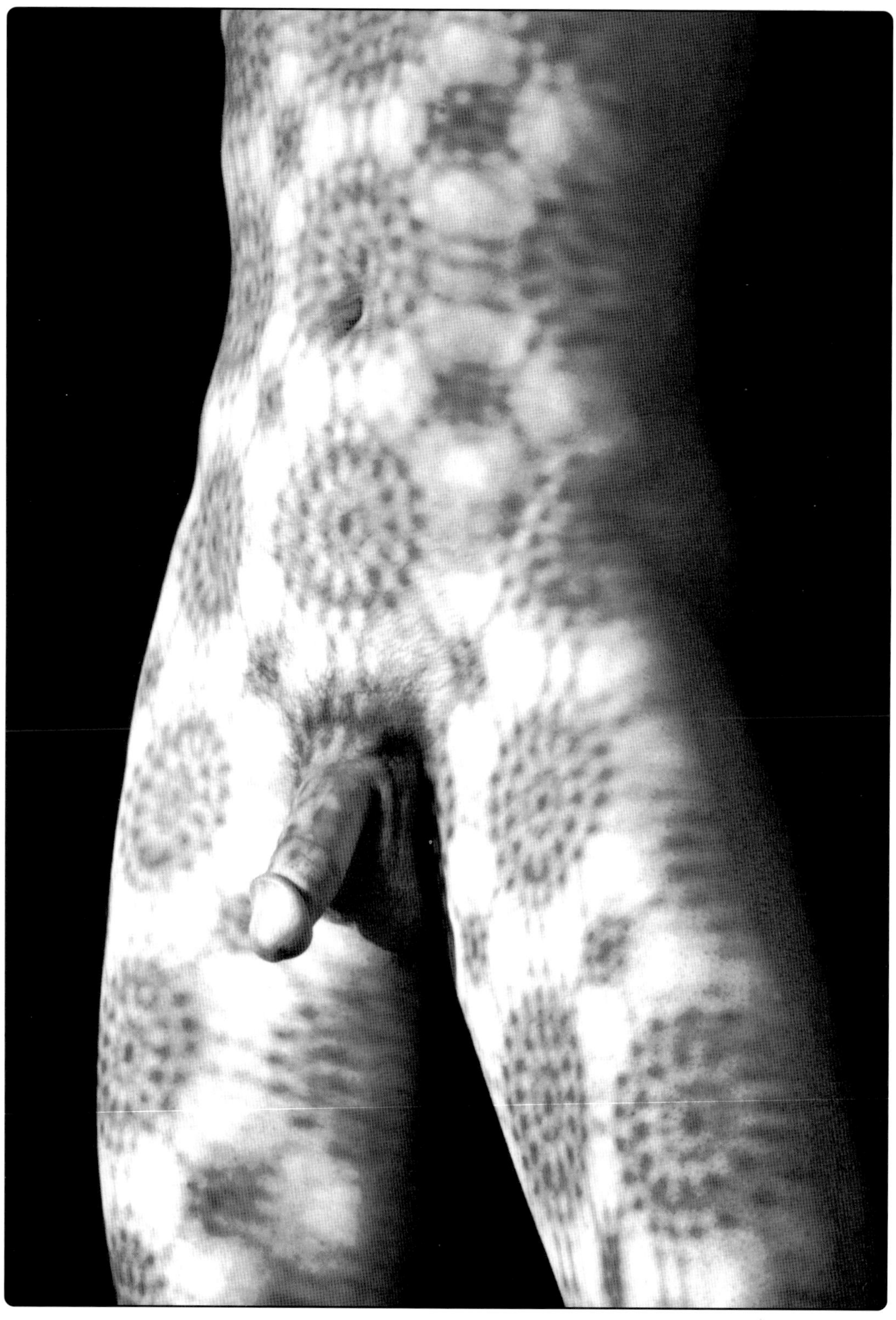

38   *Lace*   1996

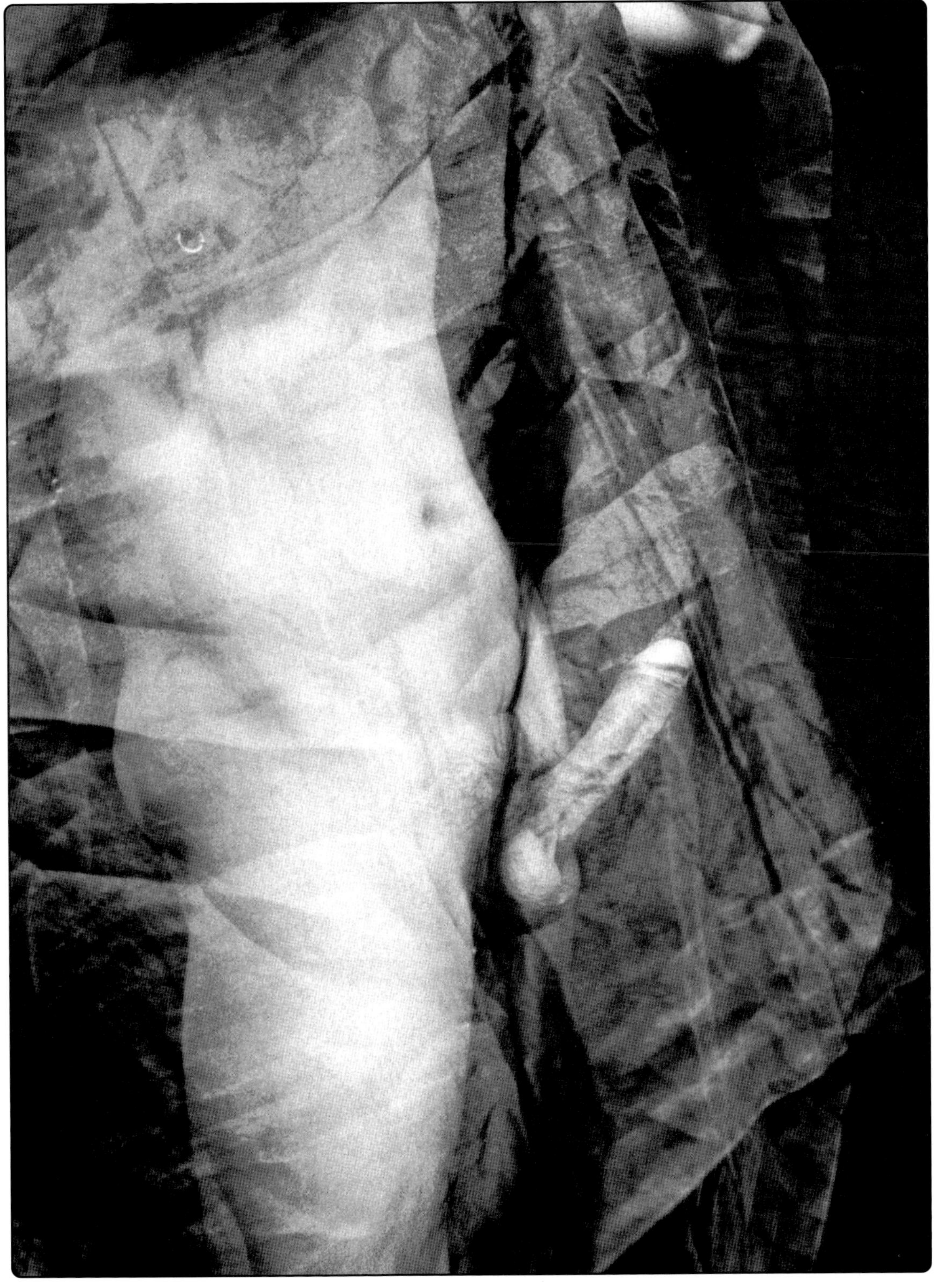

Erection   1994   39

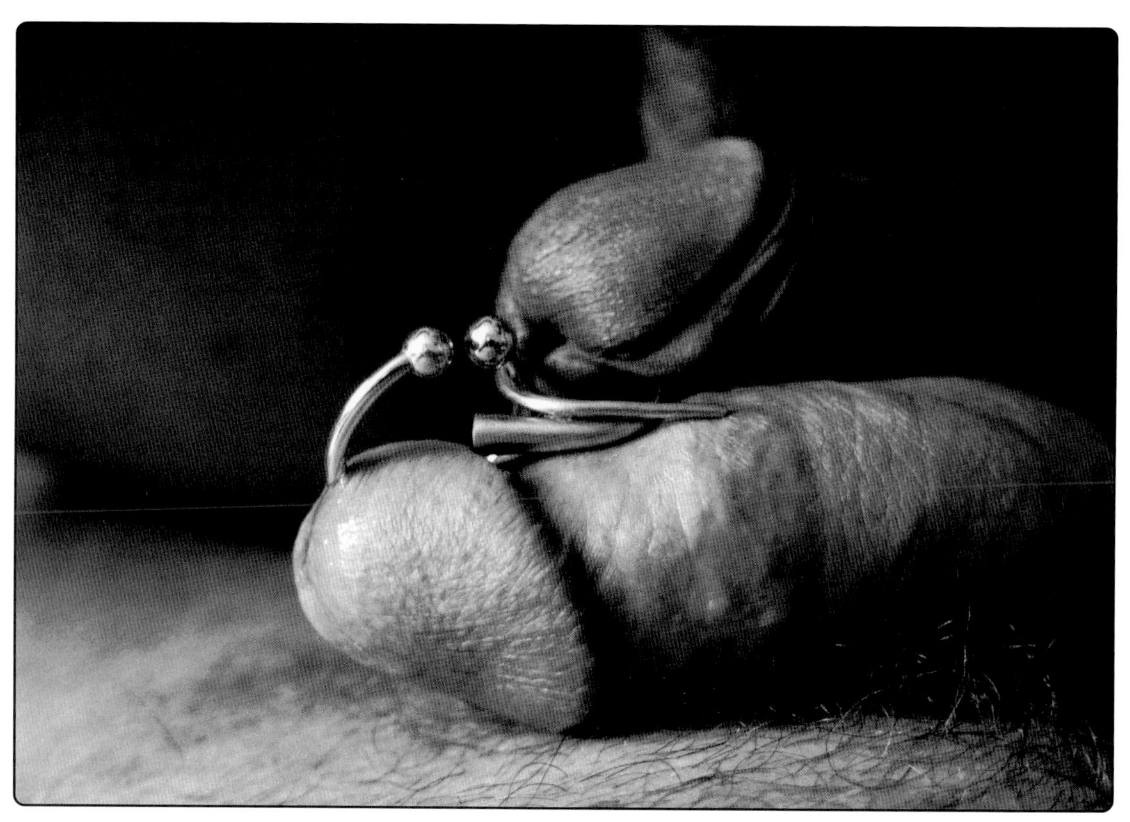

40   Link   1998

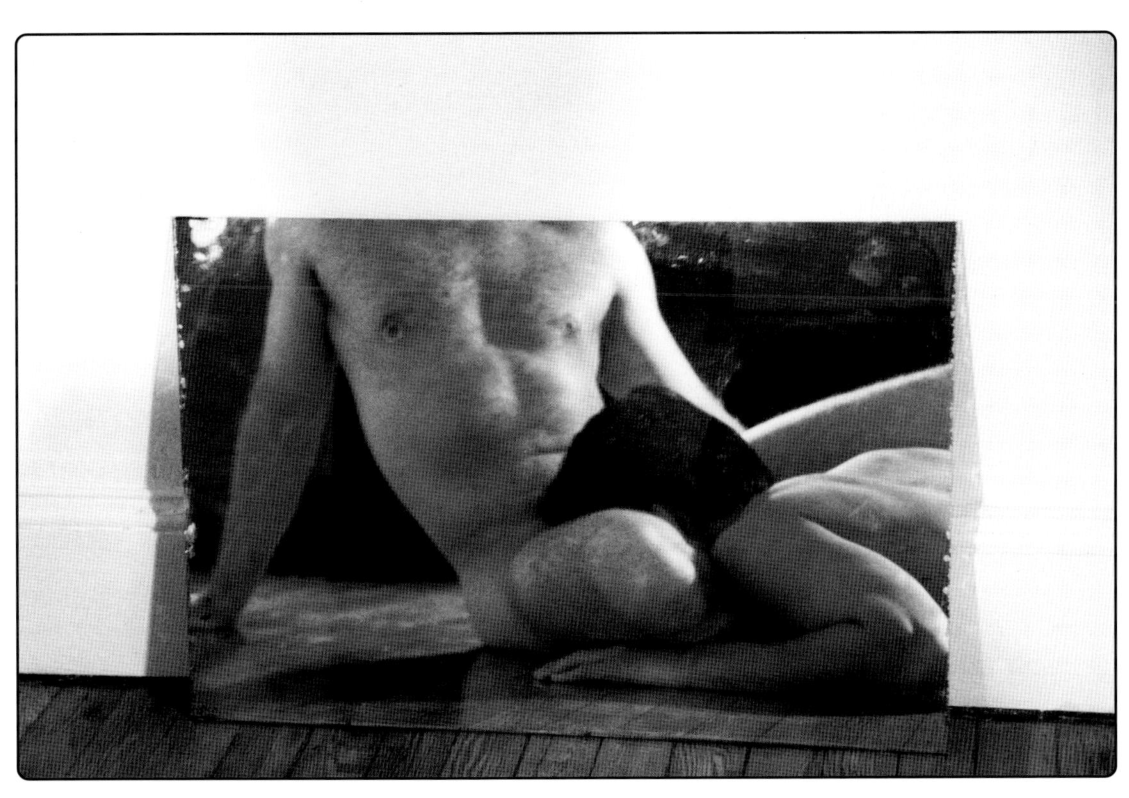

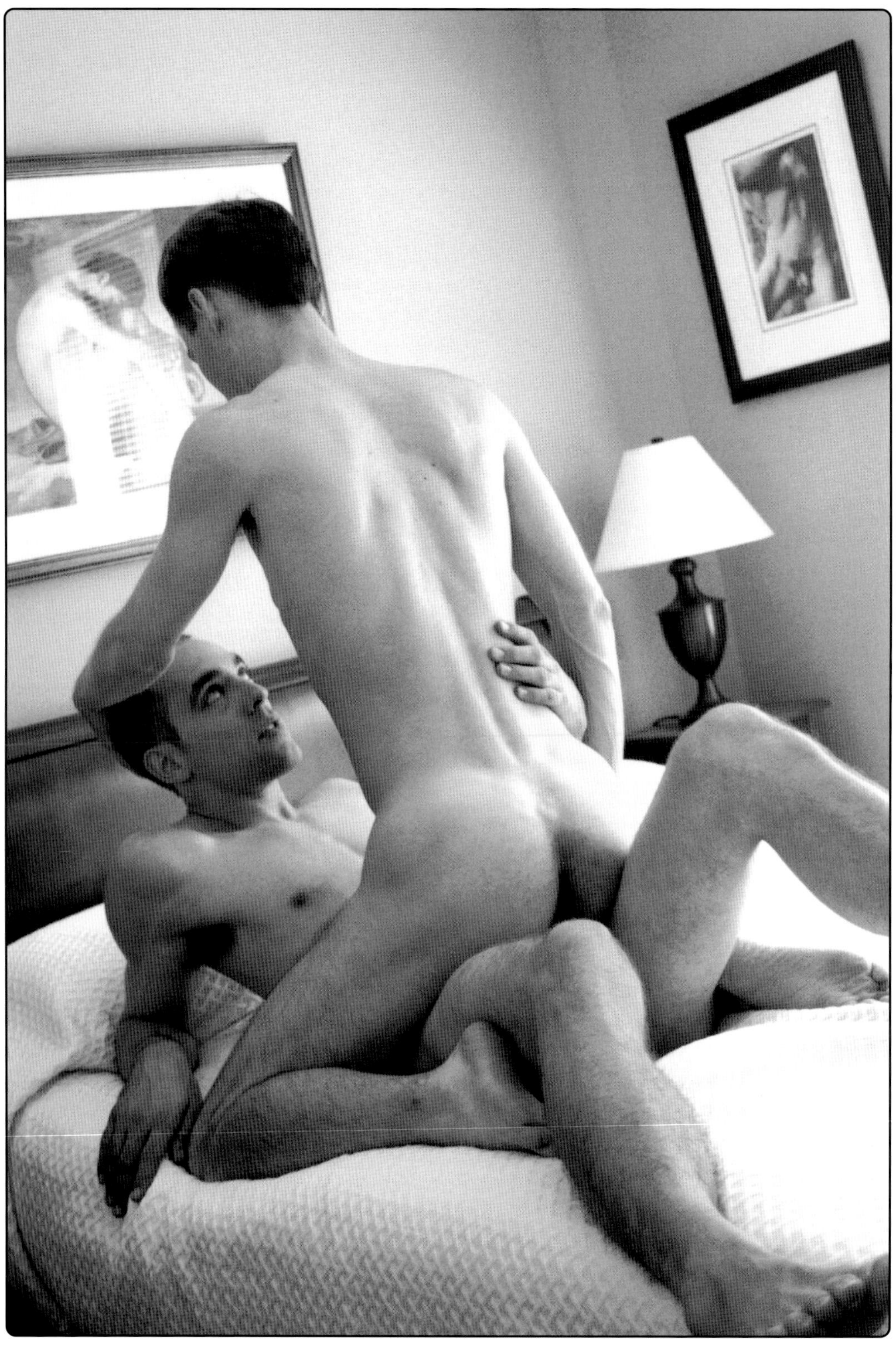

     Attraction   2000

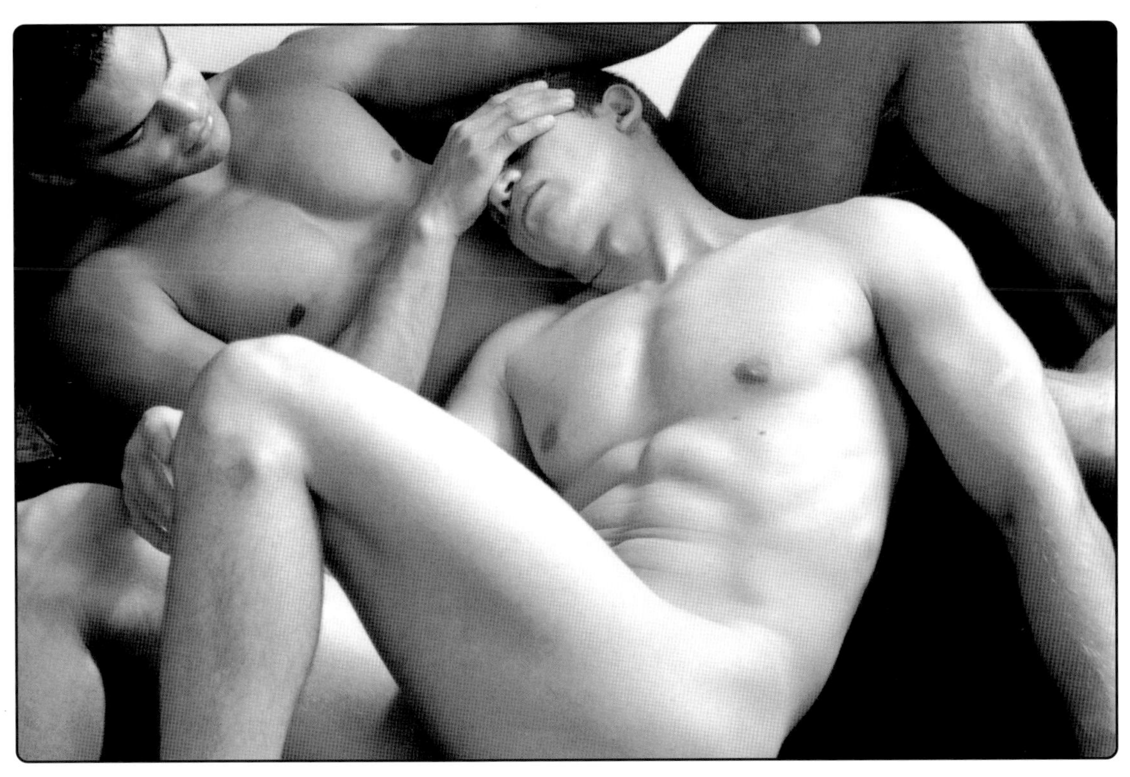

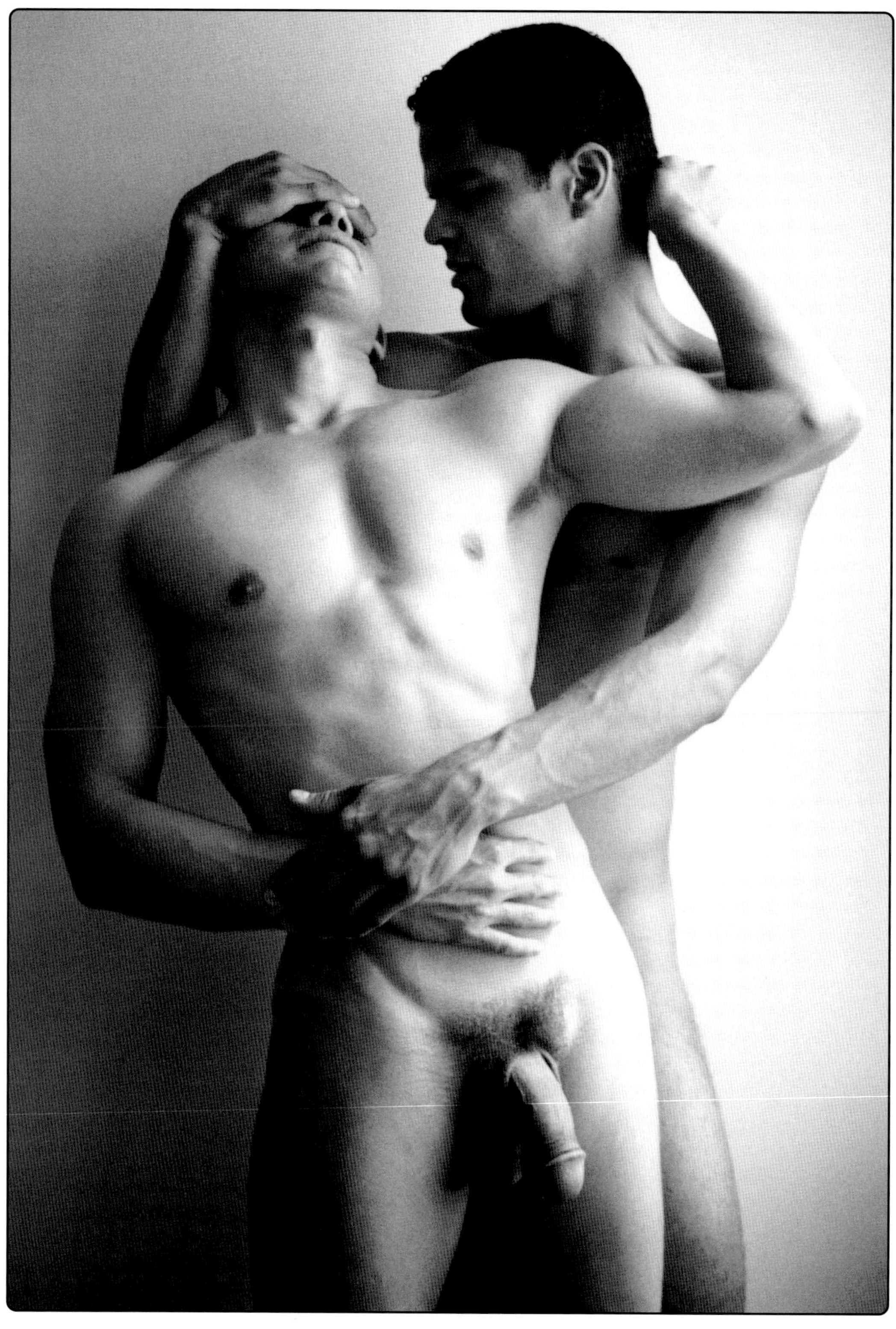

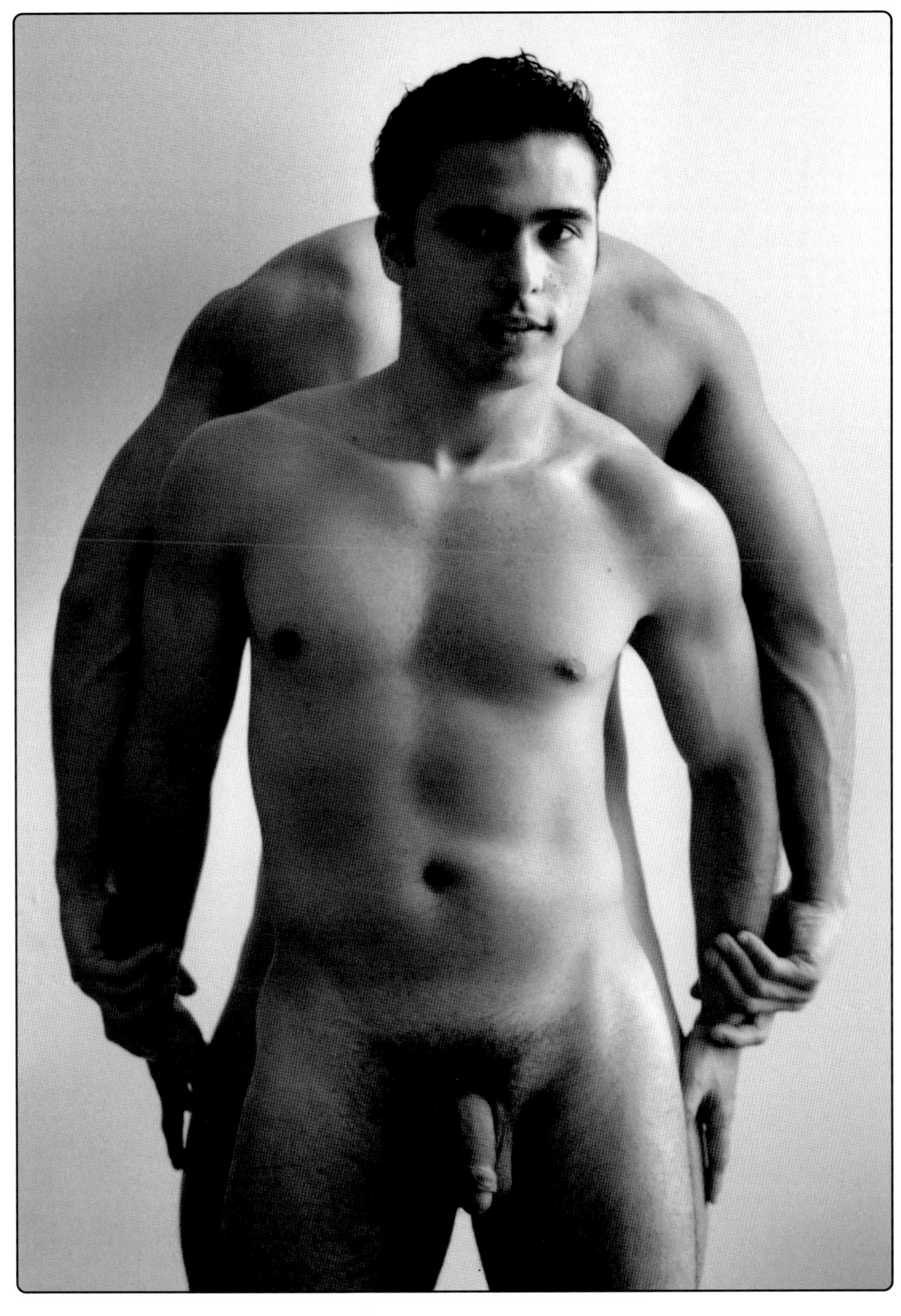

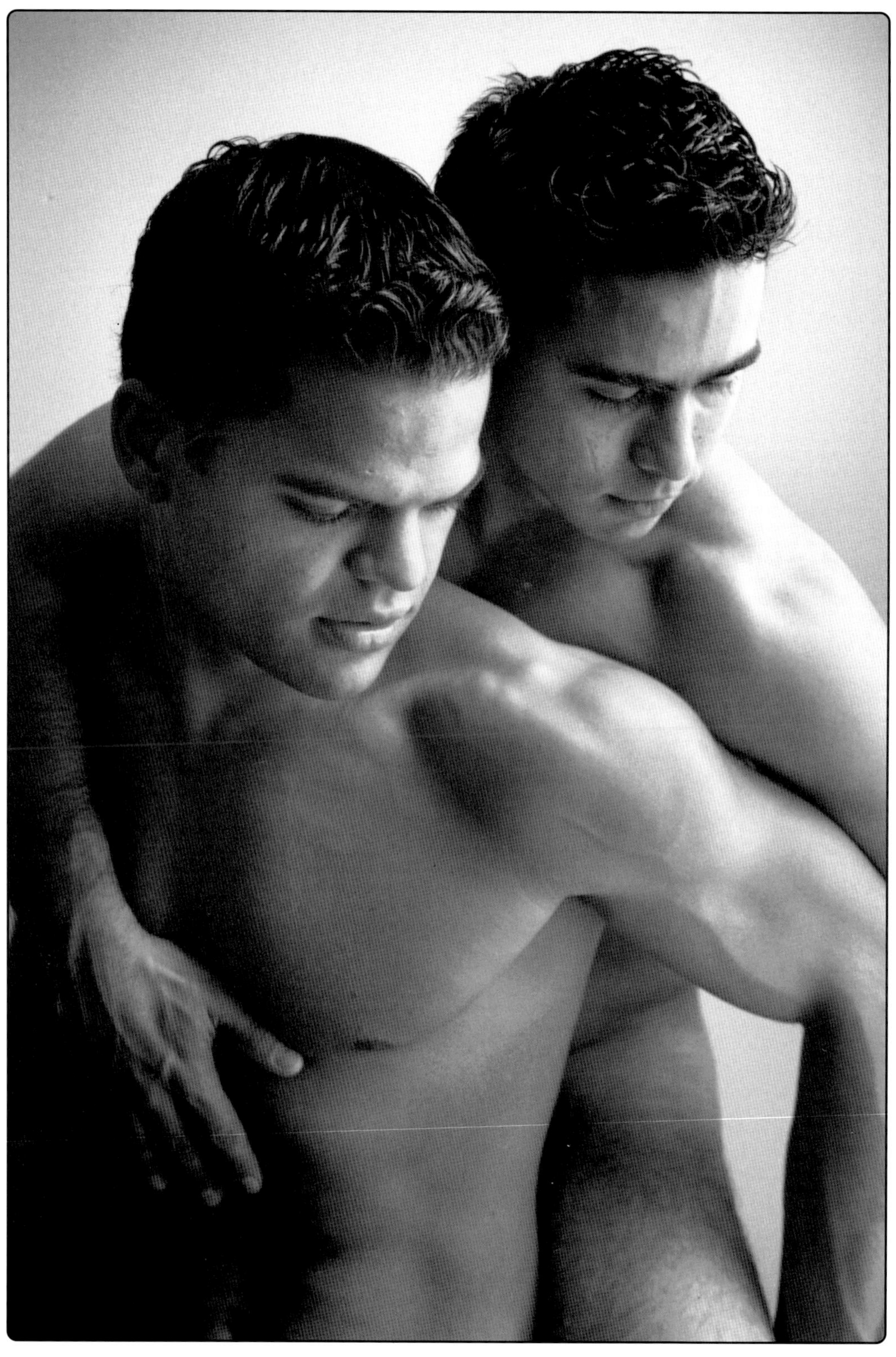

   Couple   2000

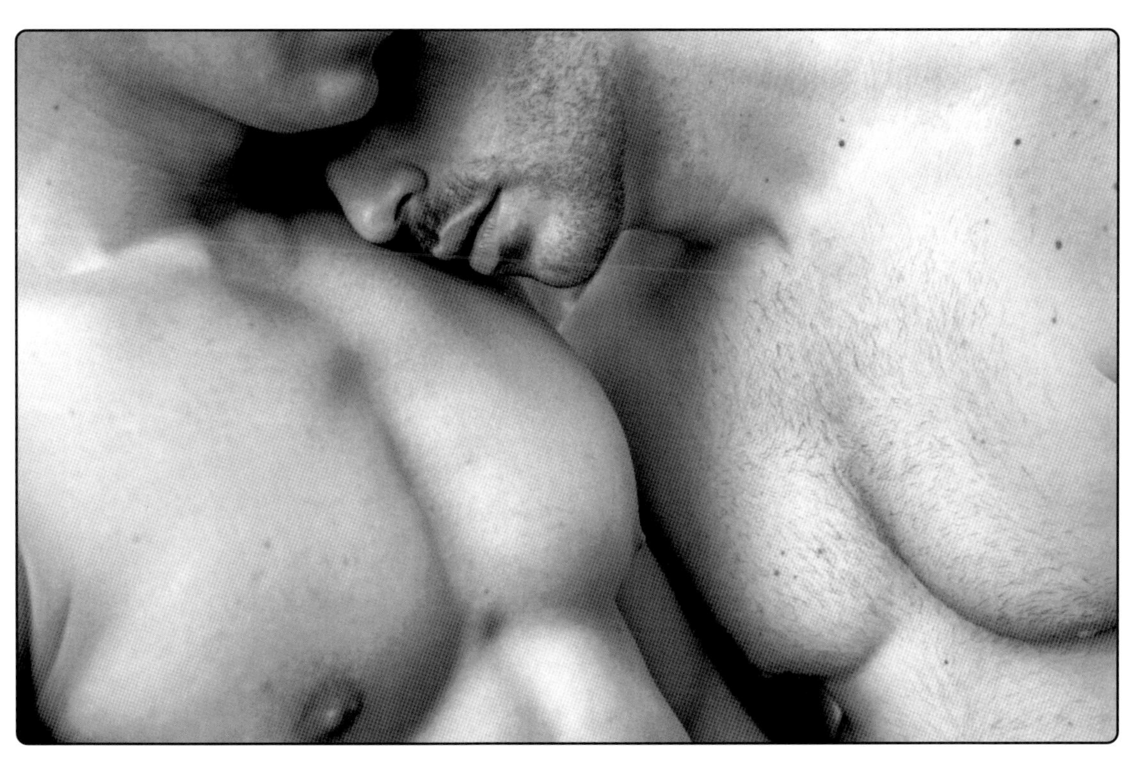

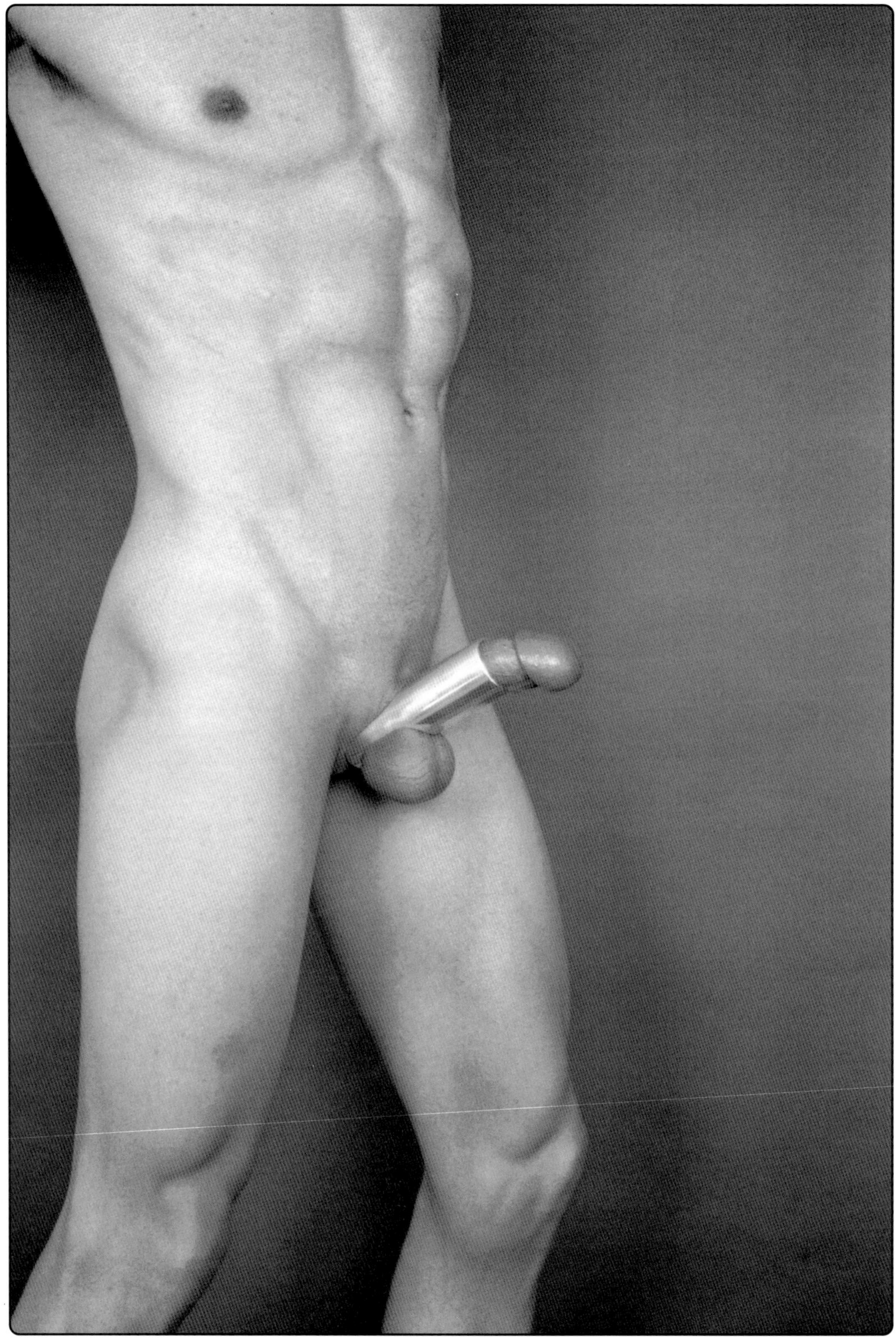

48   *Chastity   2001*

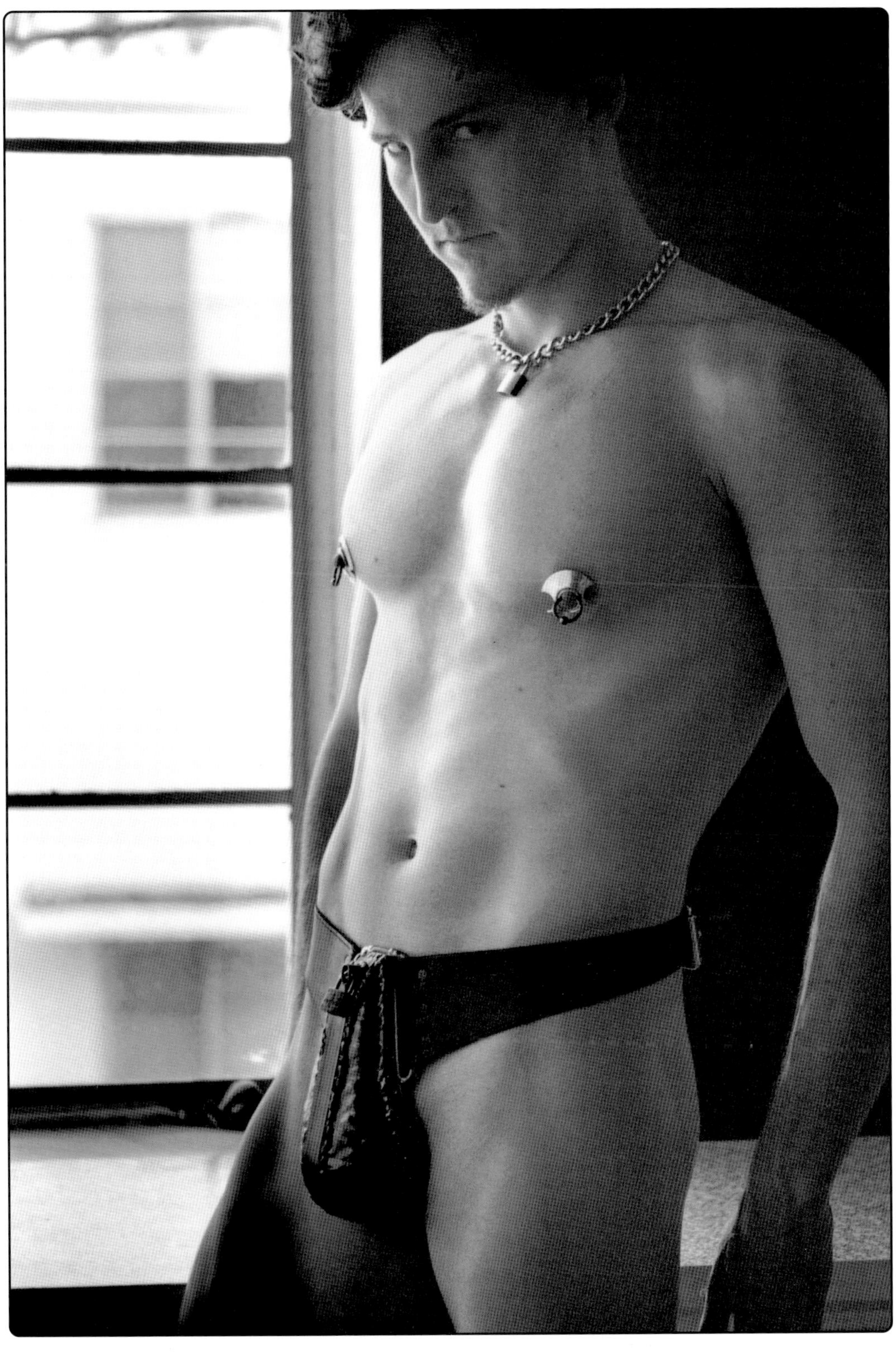

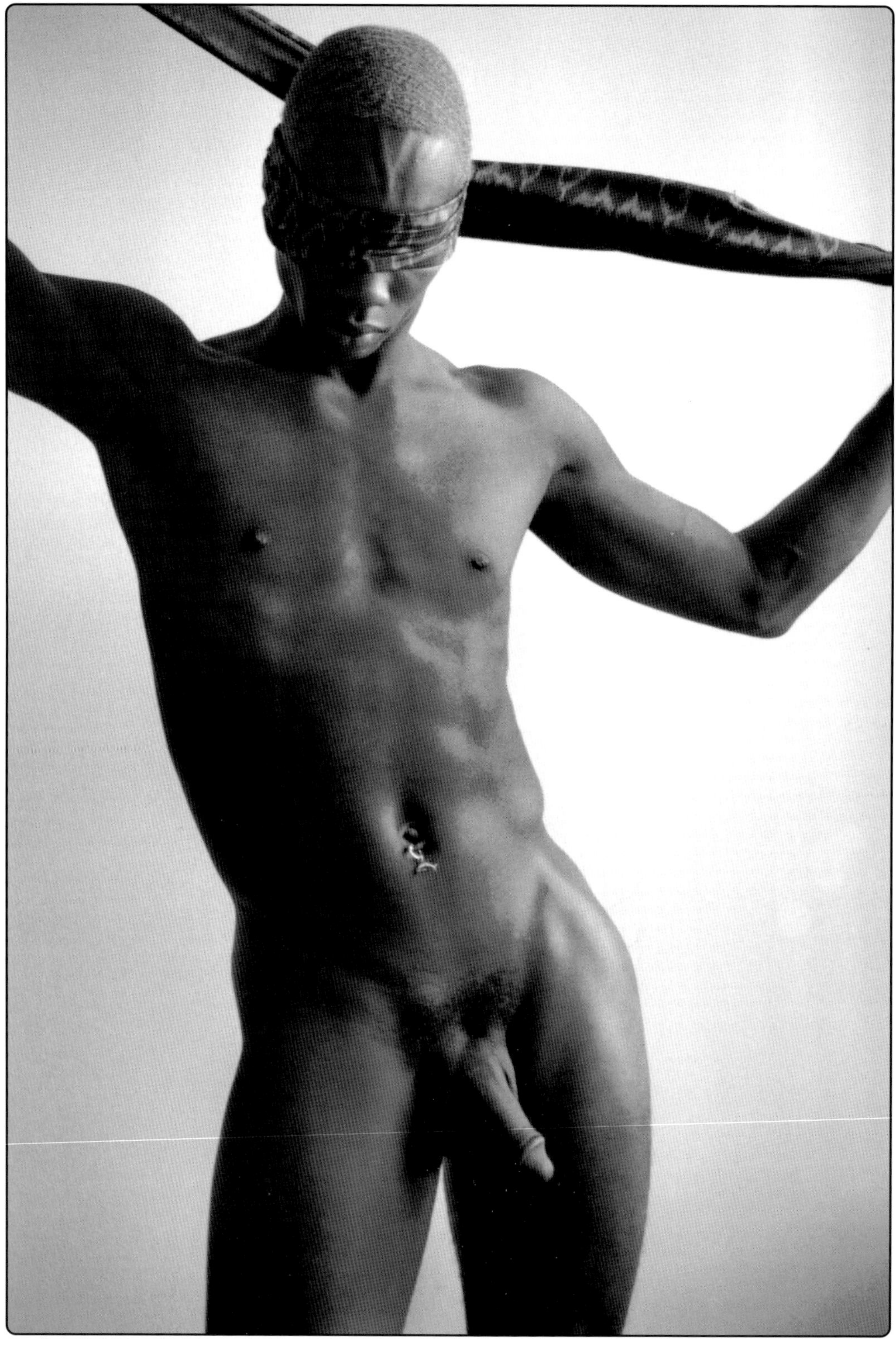

50   *Blindfold*   *2000*

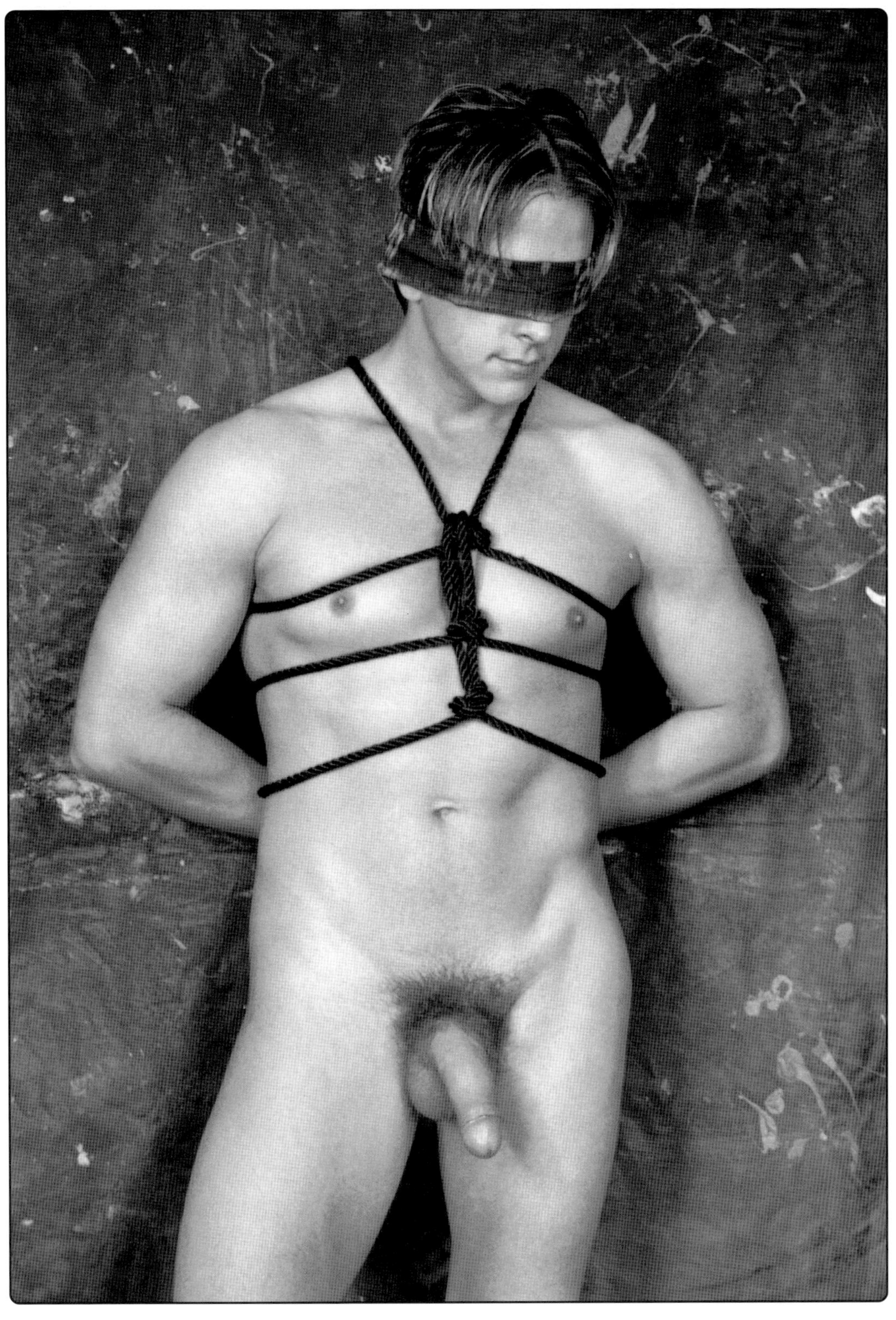

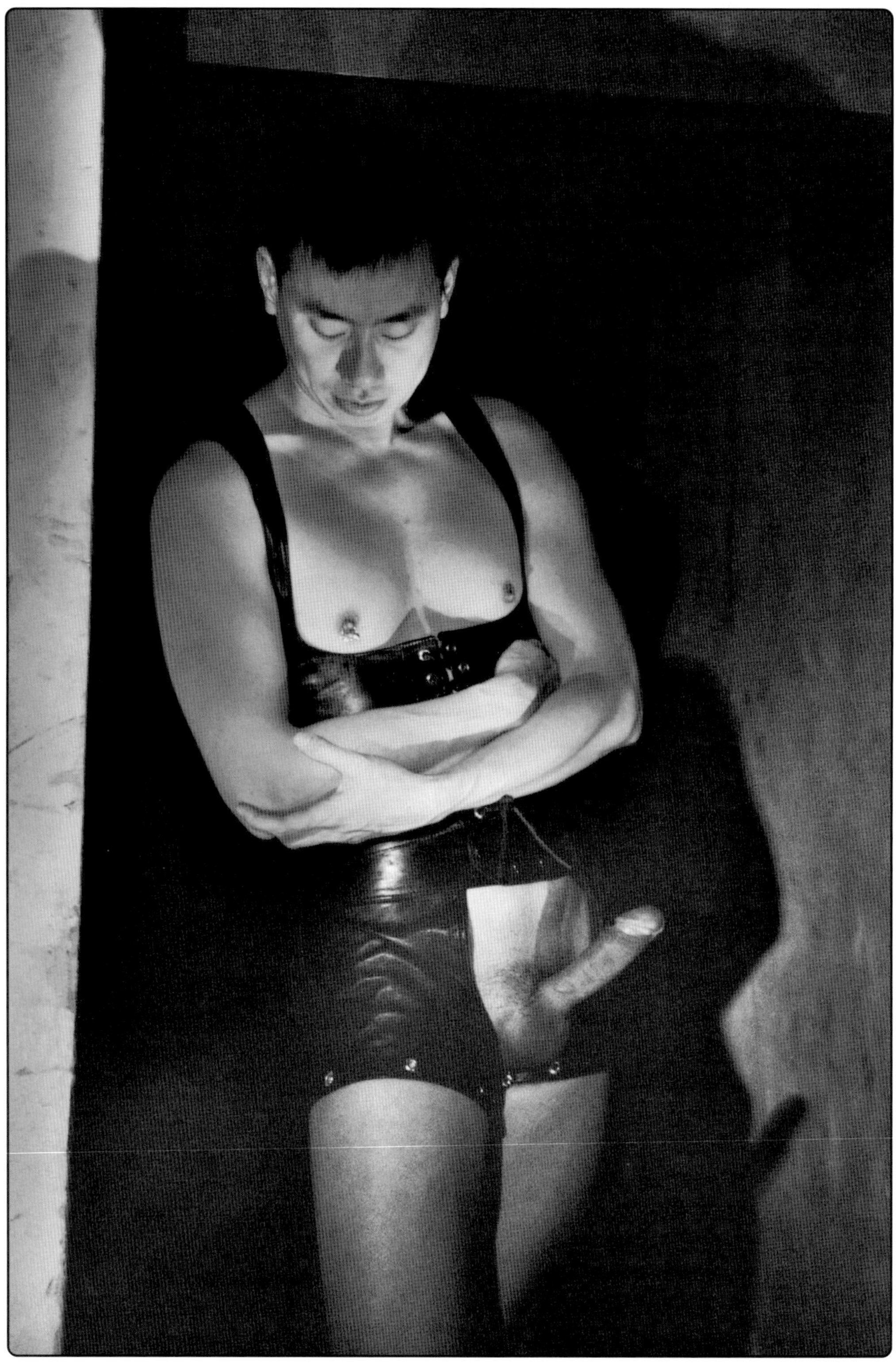

52   *Leather Boy   1994*

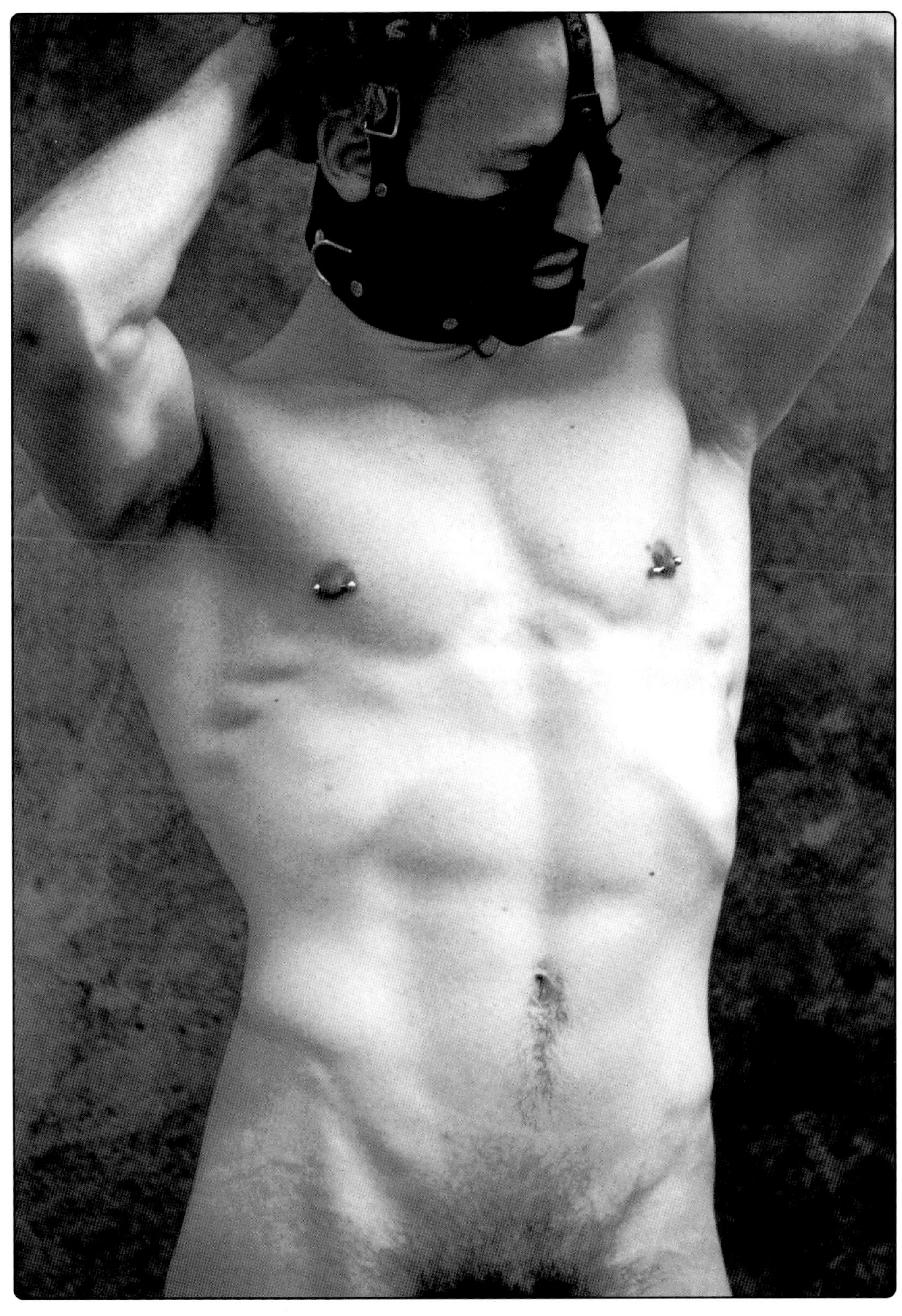

College Boy in Leather Mask   1999   53

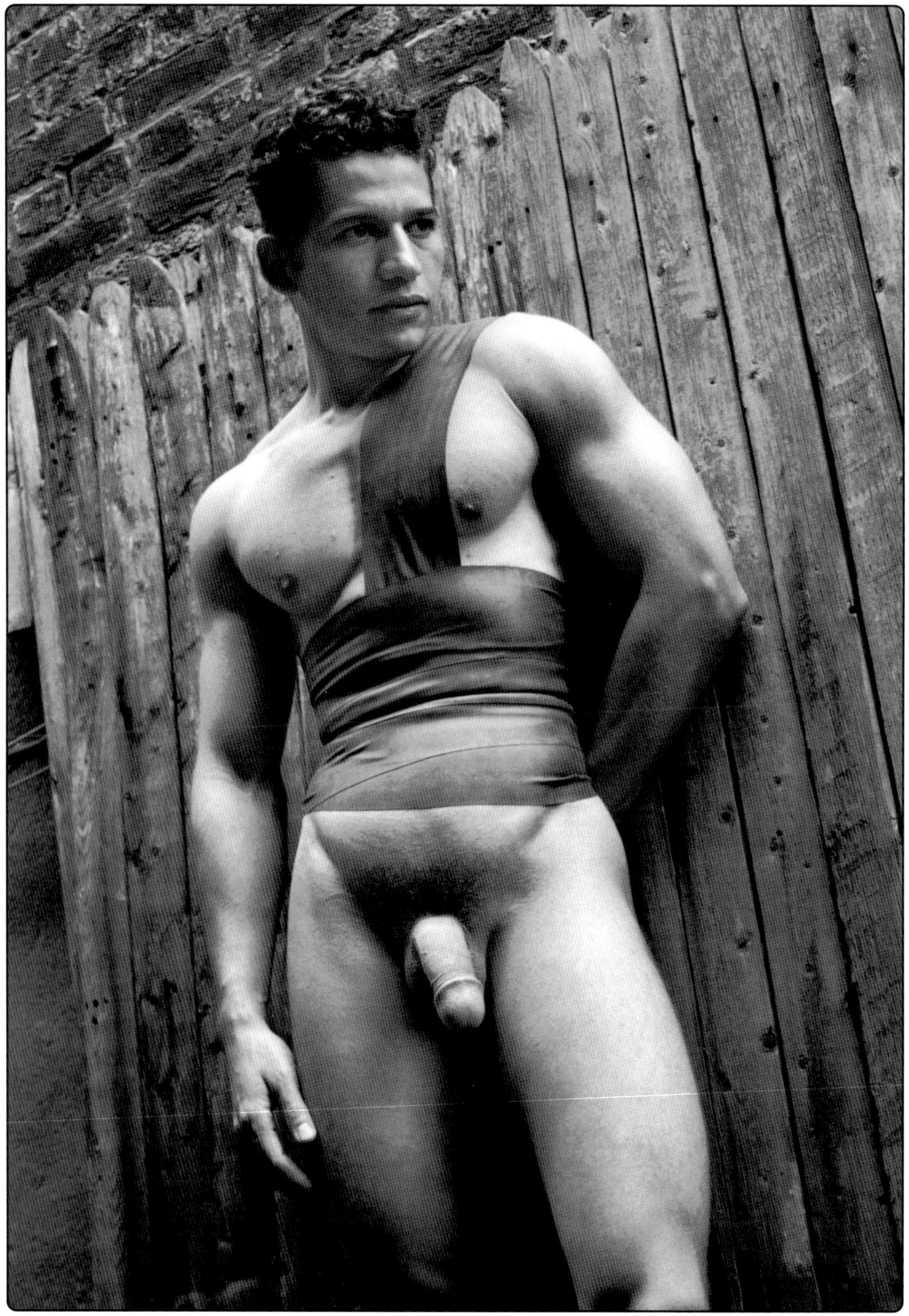

   Rubber Bandage   2000

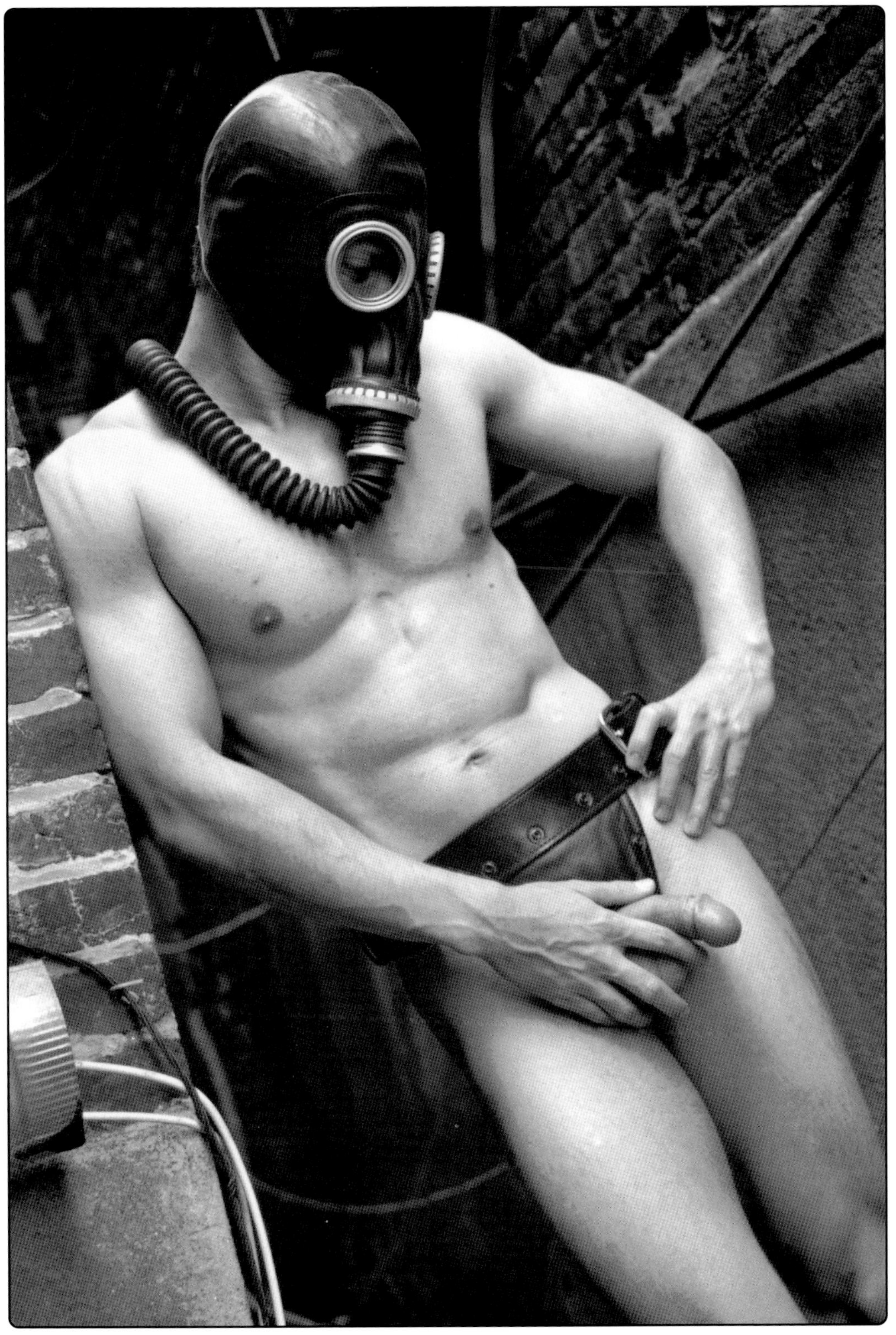

Gas Mask   2000   55

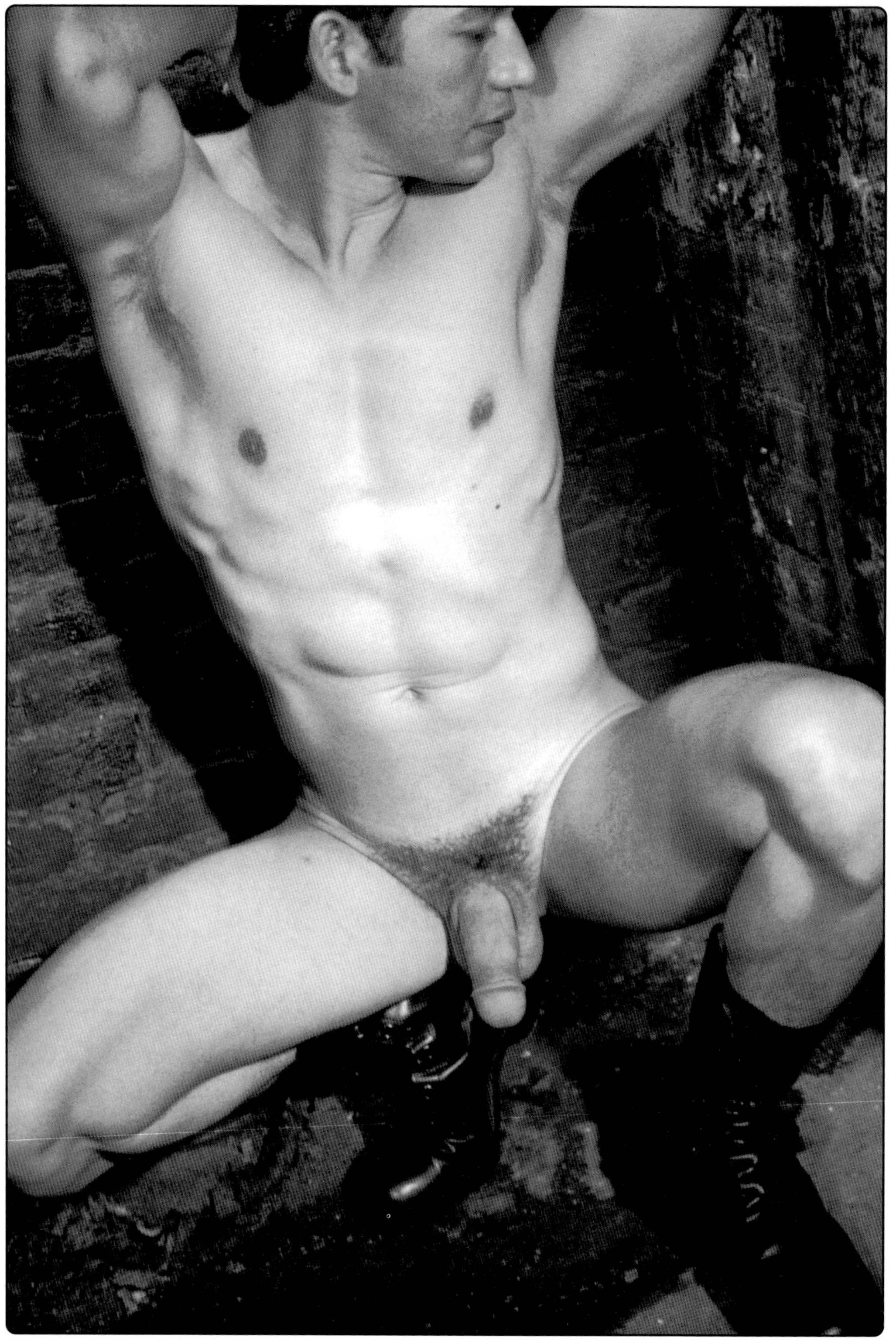

56   *Boot Boy*   *2000*

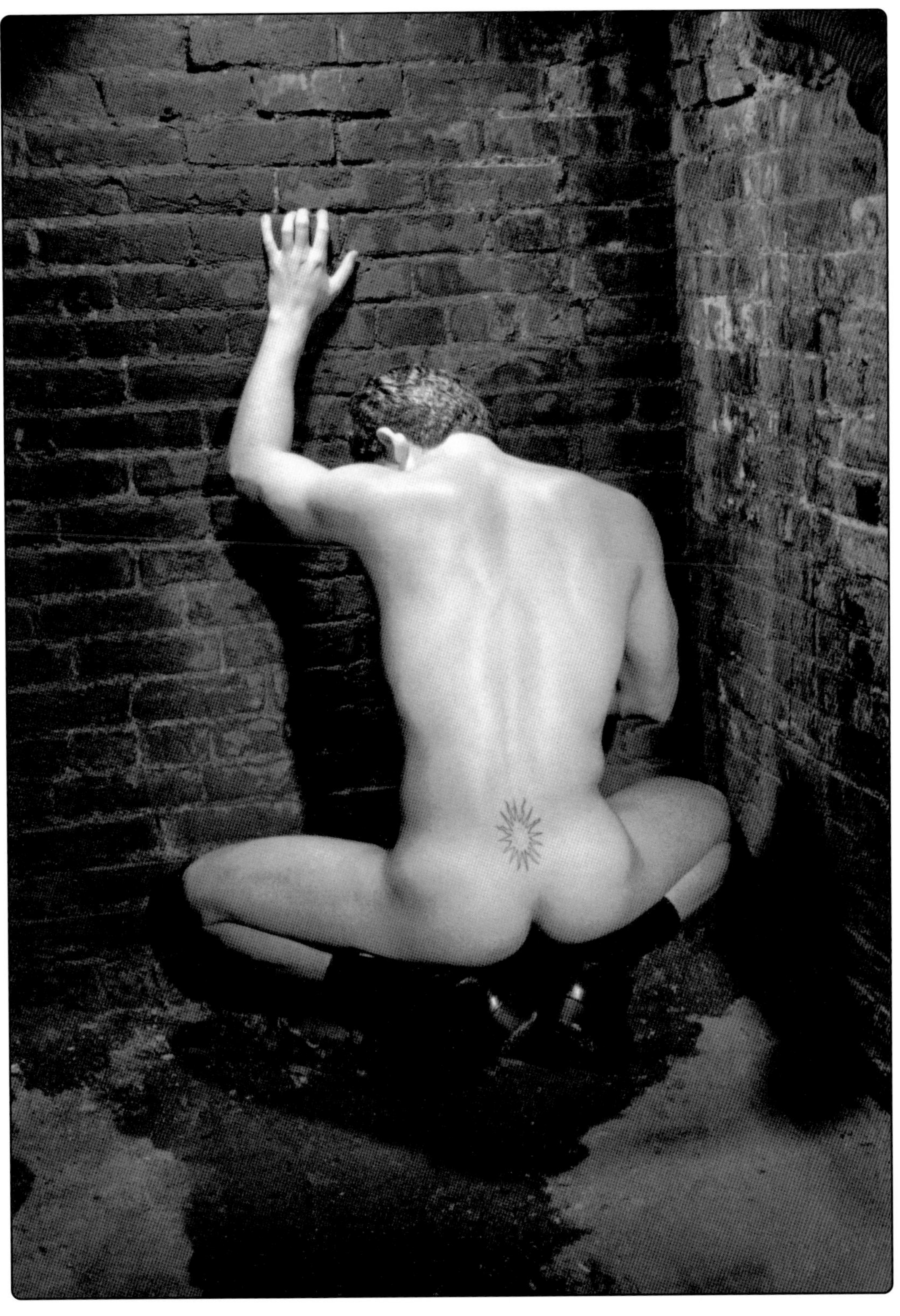

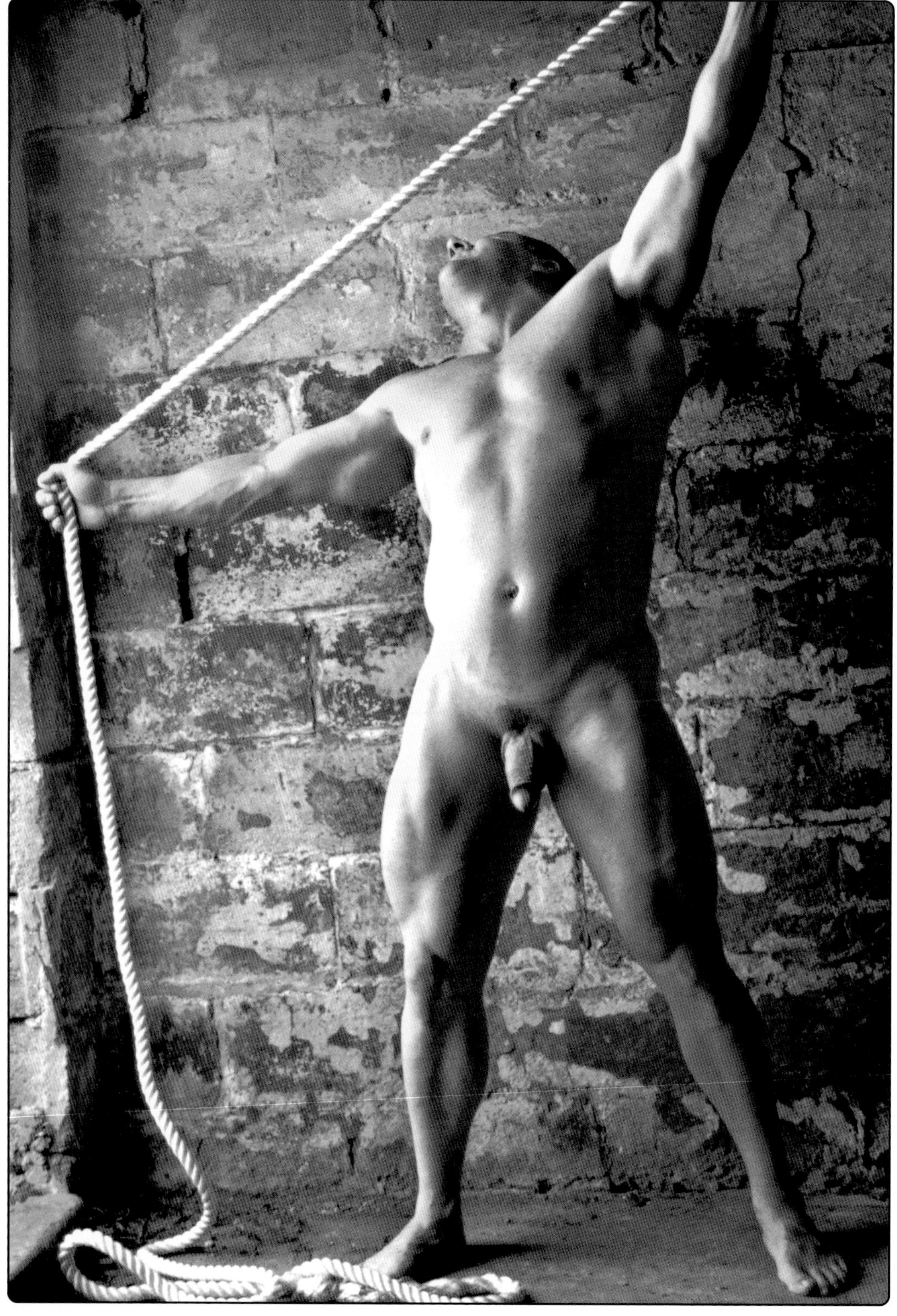

58   *Rope*   2000

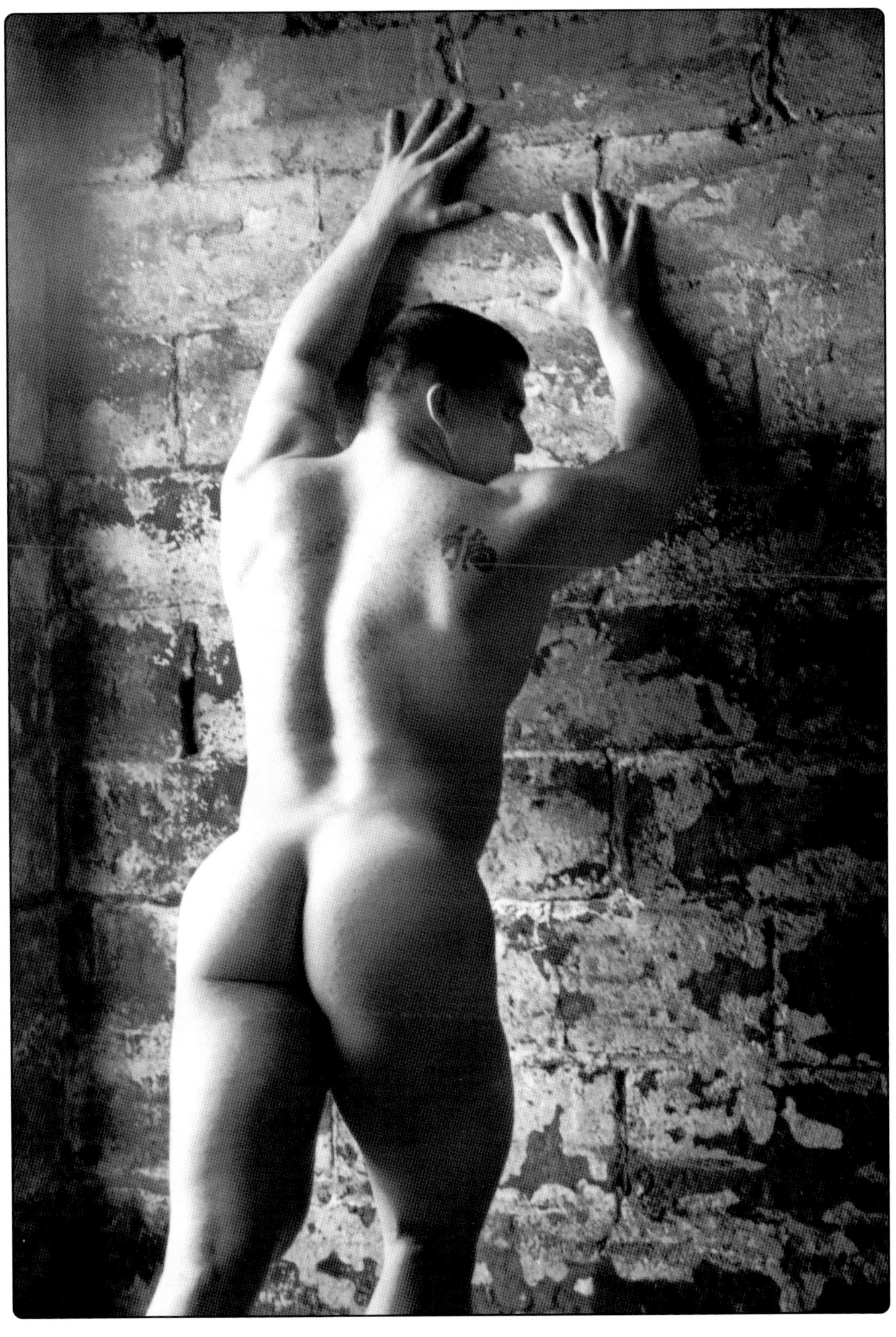

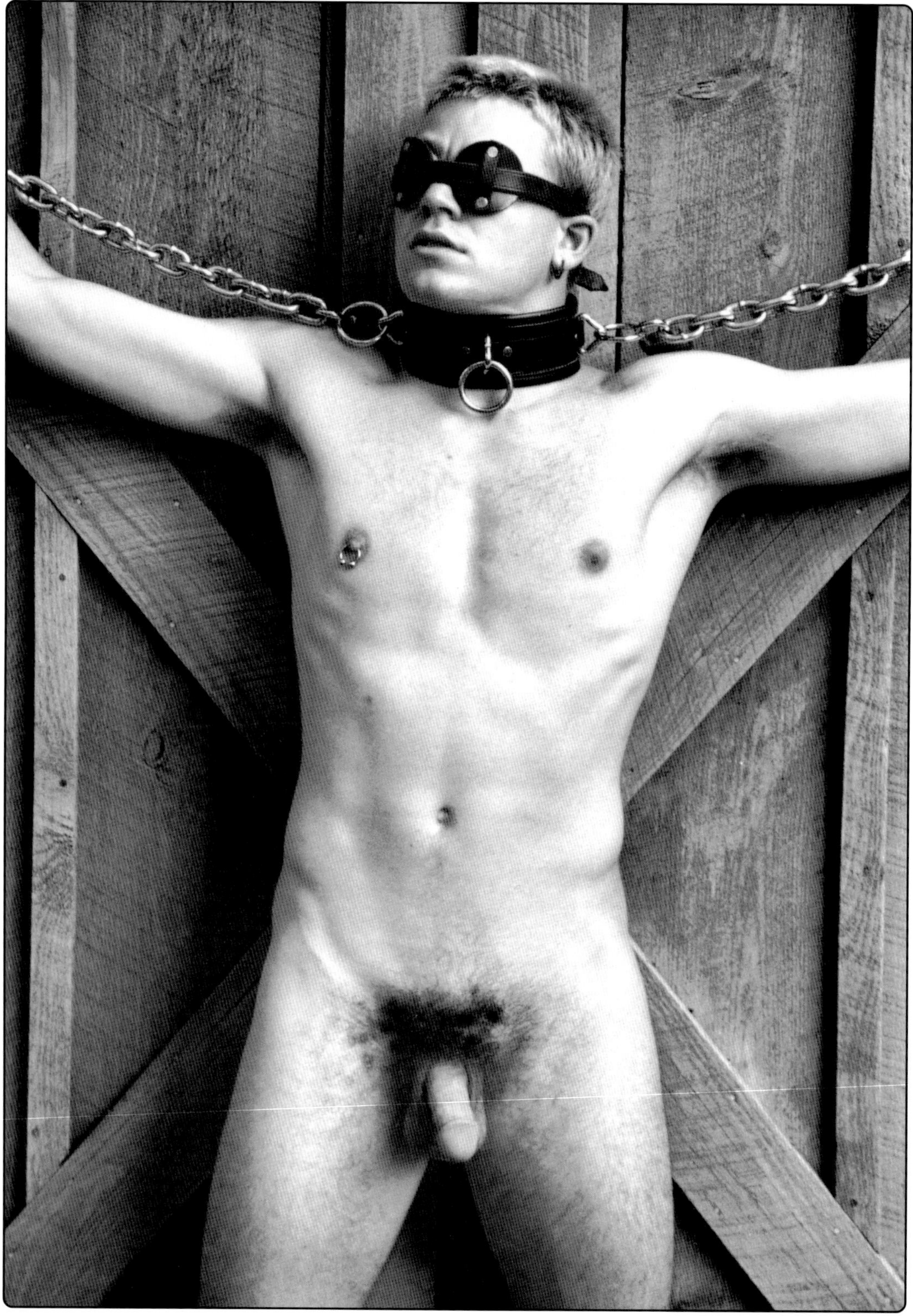

    Bad Boy   1994

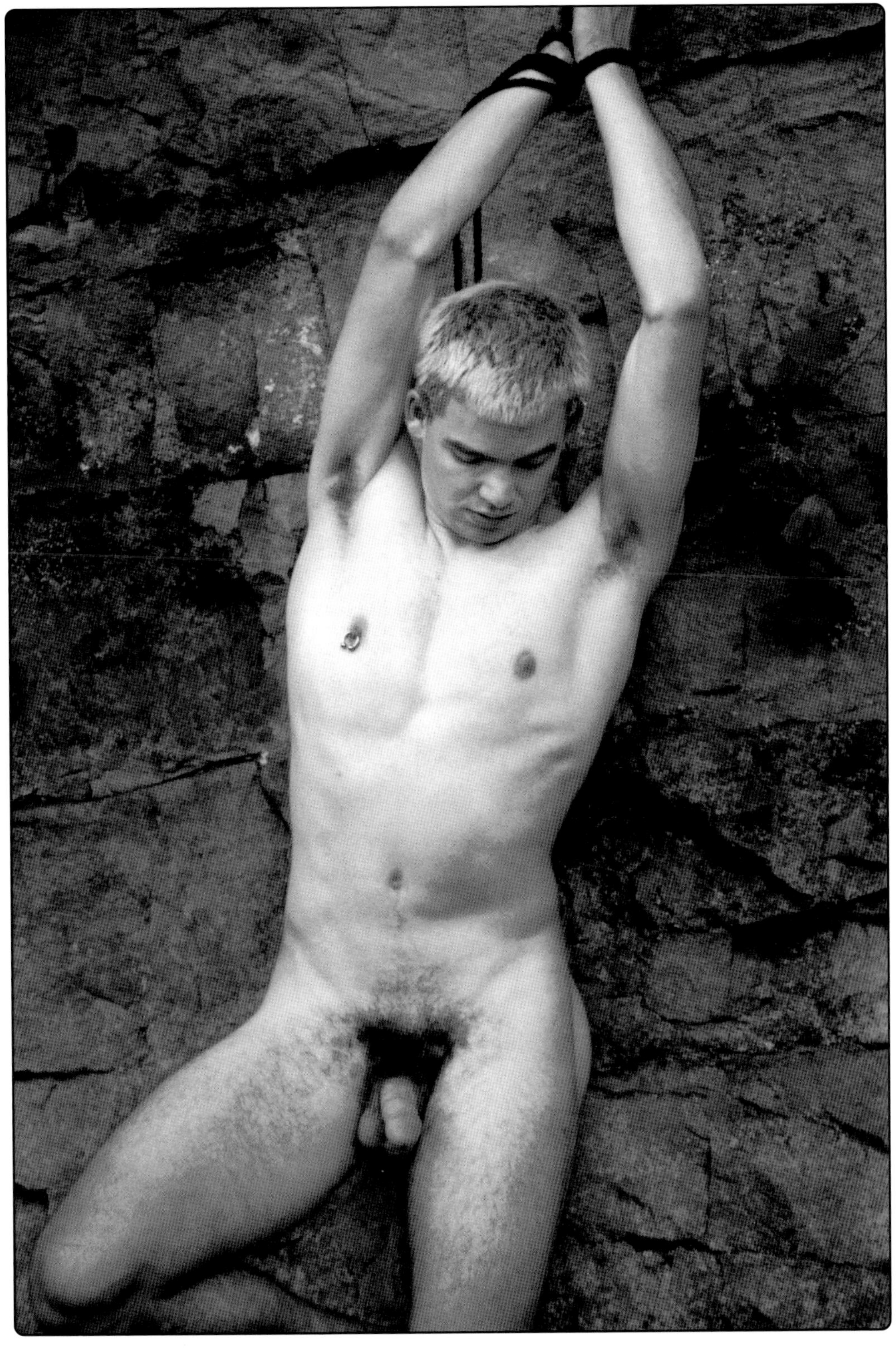

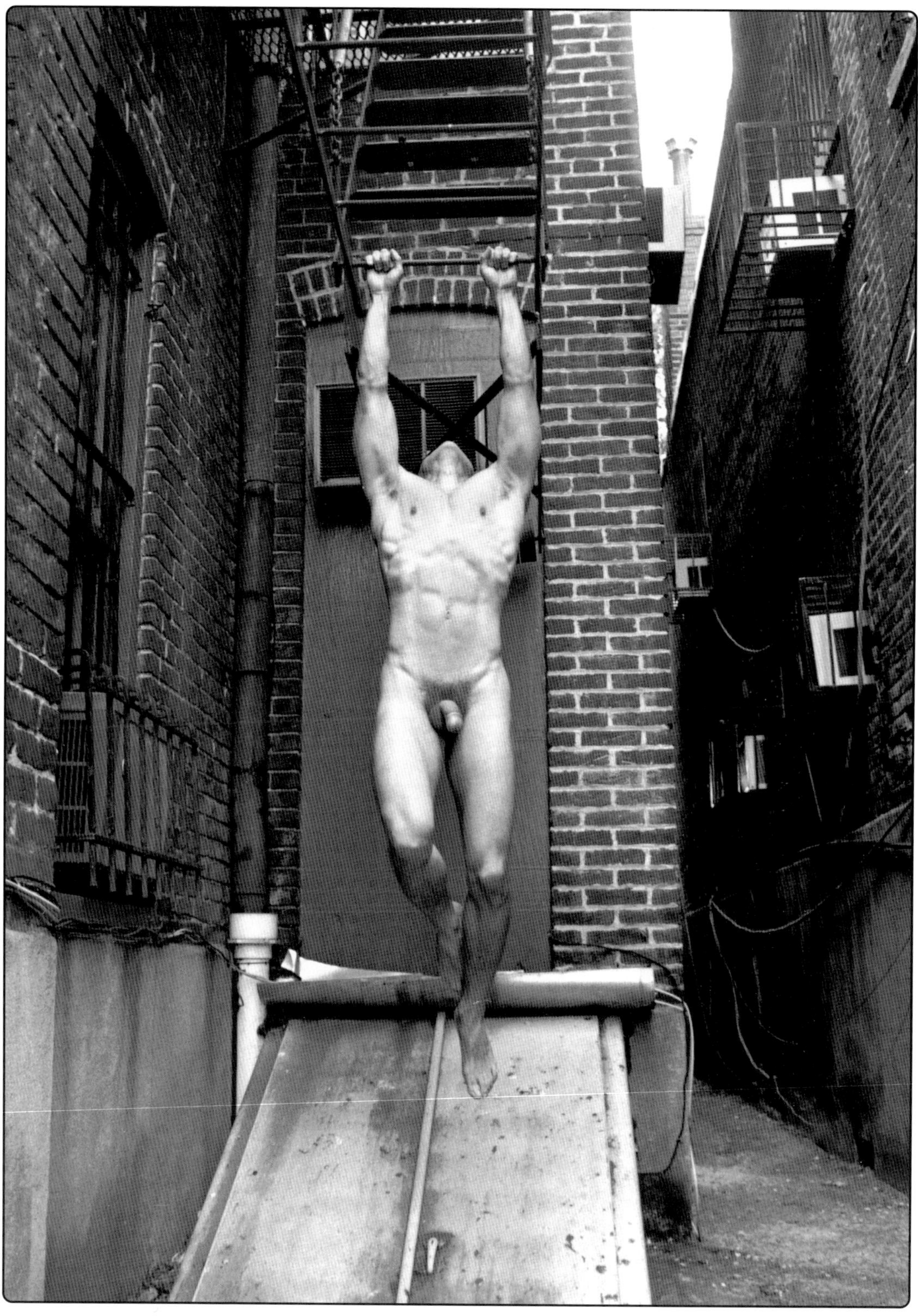

62   *Fire Escape*   *2000*

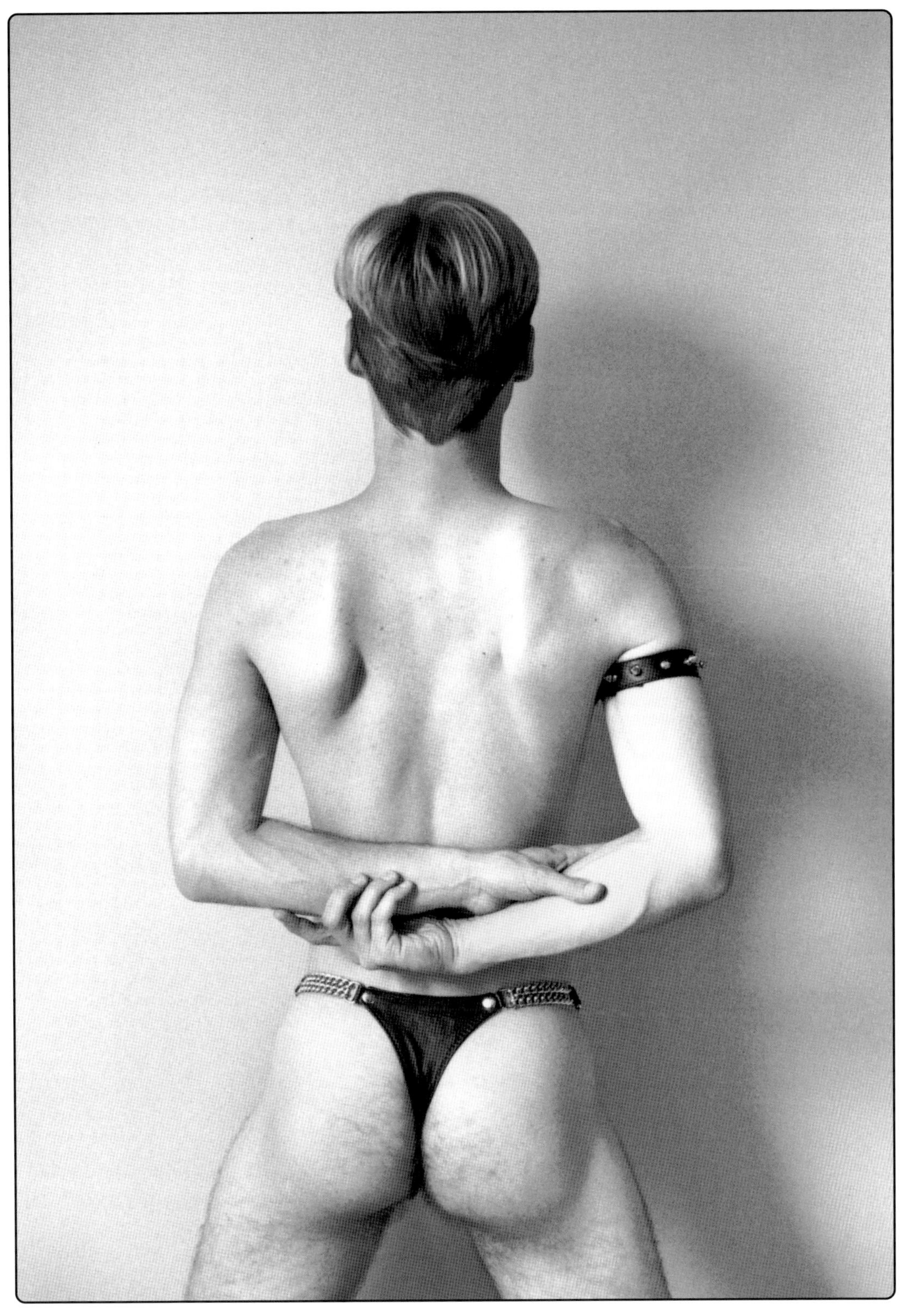

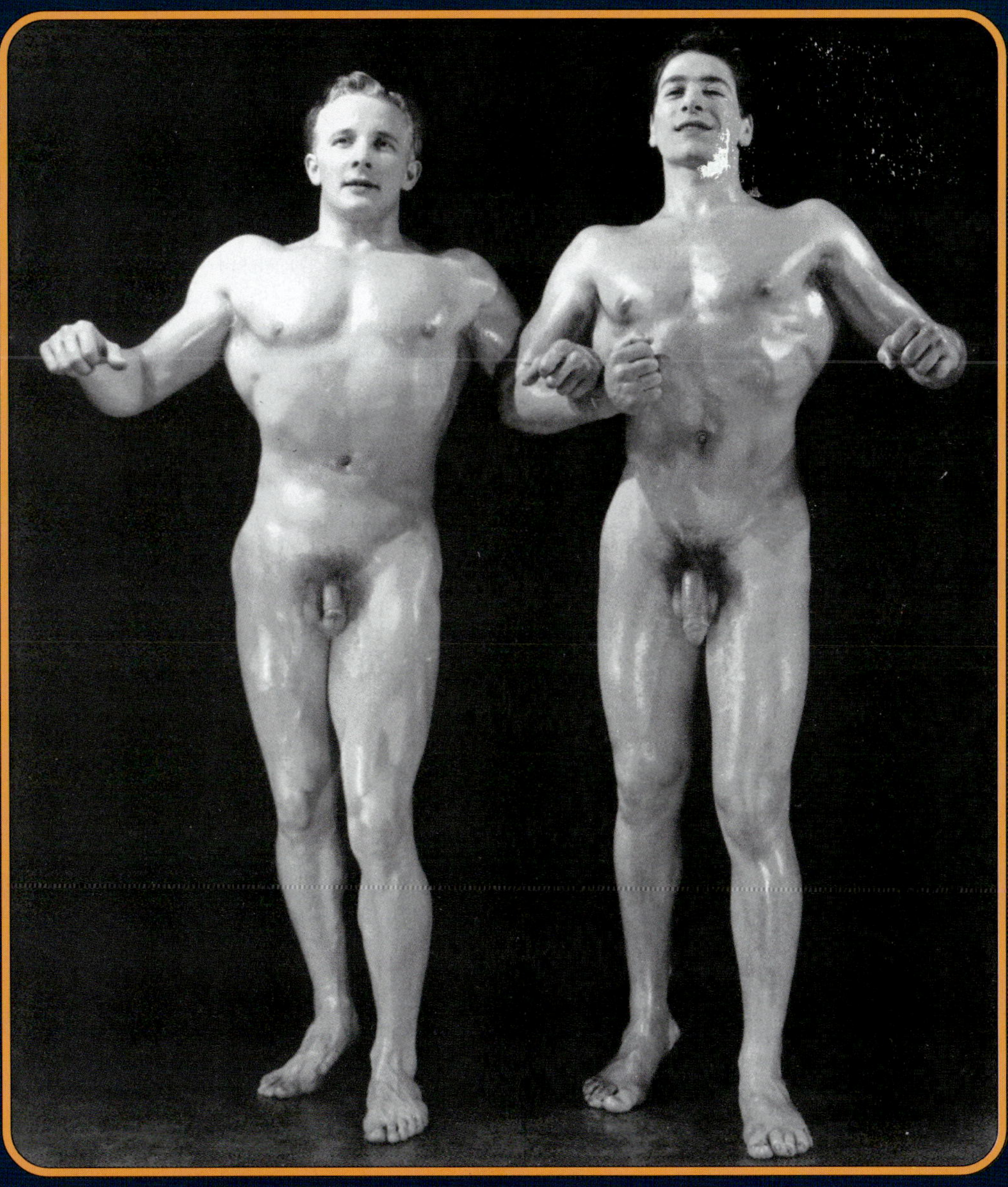

David Butt
YOUNG & HAIRY
– photos

This popular English photographer concentrates his gaze upon the younger hairy male, not muscle-bound wannabee adonis but the nice, friendly boy-next-door.

David Butt has captured something about the spirit of the age we're living in – male models nonchalantly displaying erections outdoors and indoors – and a few lads you will recognize from **The English Country Lad.**

(64 pages, 232 x 170mm, 60 b/w plates)
ISBN 0 85449 292 5   concise format softback
EU UK£15.95 US $25 AUS $30   **OCT 99**

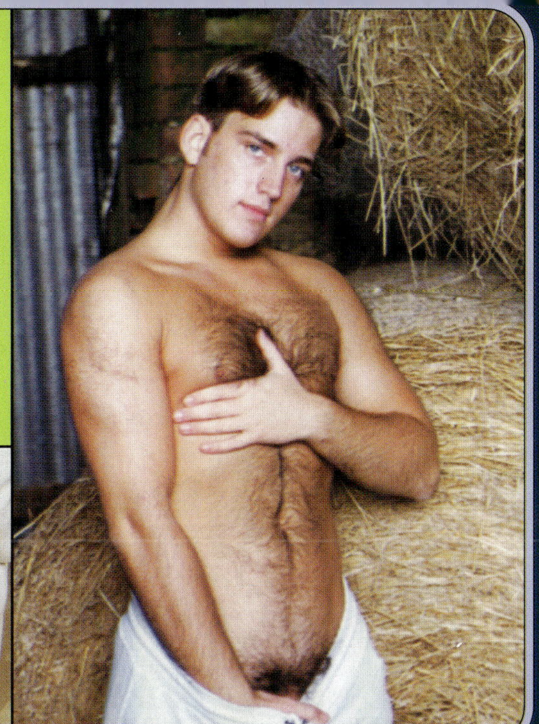

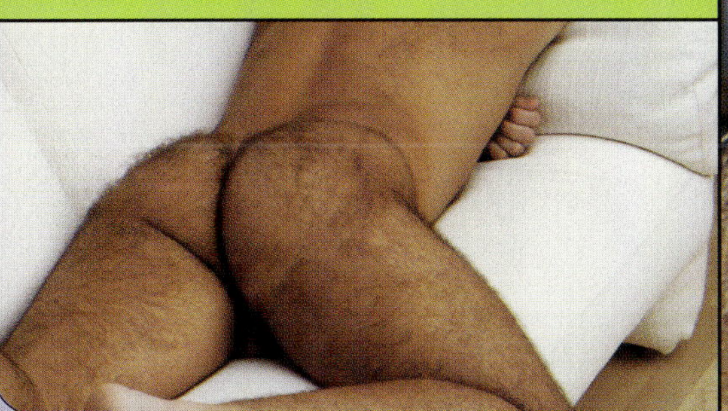

David Butt
THE ENGLISH COUNTRY LAD

These lovely photos focus English country lads not town guys. Butt's lads are free and easy, open and friendly not mean and cruel. They love to pose naked or partly clad on the farm, in the field, in thicket and wood enjoying the freedom that only nature provides.

(64 pages, 232 x 170mm, 16 b/w, 44 color plates)
ISBN 0 85449 239 9   concise format softback
EU UK£15.95 US $24.95 AUS $29.95

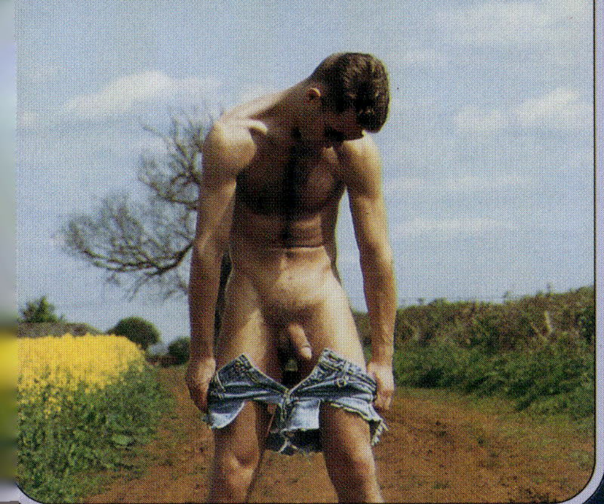

David Chapman (ed)
ADONIS – THE MALE PHYSIQUE
PIN-UP, 1870-1940

The photohistory of the male nude pin-up from the classic fin-de-siècle statuesque pose of the first musclemen to 1940's wasp-waisted Hollywood boys. David Chapman's introduction is on the evolution of the male body beautiful.

(108 pages, 255 x 228mm, 100 b/w plates)
ISBN 0 85449 250 X   medium format softback
EU UK£20   US $30   AUS $40

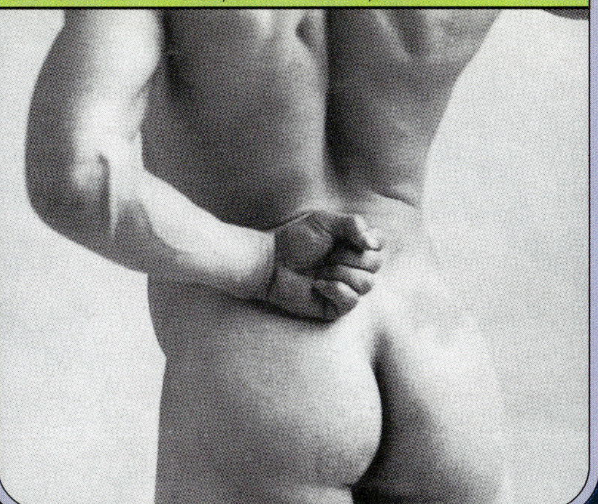

David Hutter (1935-1990)
NUDES AND FLOWERS

This English painter was a complete master of water-colour, this volume gathers together his finest male nude studies interspersed with gentle flower paintings.
(96 pages, 200 x 200mm, 40 color plates)
ISBN 907040 31 4   concise format softback
EU   UK£9.50 AUS $19.95 not USA

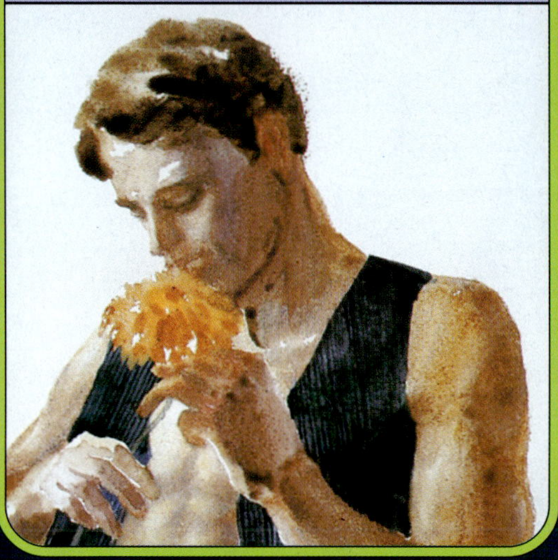

Cornelius McCarthy
INTERIORS

These paintings abound with decorative homoerotic sensuality using a palette which is subtle, vivid and quite wild. Well-hung beautifully proportioned male models in outdoor and interior settings.
(64 pages, 200 x 200mm, 40 color plates)
ISBN 0 85449 015 9   concise format softback
EU UK£8.95   AUS $19.95 not USA
 (also in hardback , see order form)

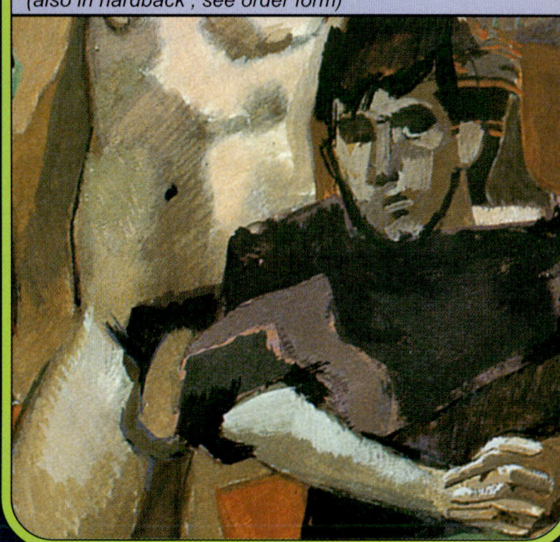

J.B. Harter
ENCOUNTERS WITH
THE NUDE MALE

The New Orleans artist neo-classicly expresses the essence of the gay world where males parade as males in search of other males.
(64 pages, 232 x 170mm, 40 color plates)
ISBN 0 85449 245 3   concise format hardback
EU UK£20   US $30   AUS $40

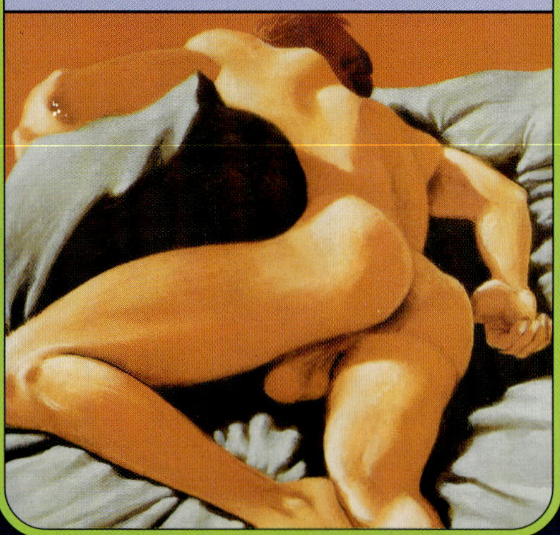

R. D. Riccoboni
RAINBOW NATION

This Los Angeles gay painter captures an urban gay world westcoast style. Highly optimistic, vividly colorful – gay rodeo, pride demonstrations, male to male love scenes – our lives.
(64 pages, 255 x 228mm, 40 color plates)
ISBN 0 85449 240 2   medium format softback
EU UK£9.95 US $14.95 AUS $19.95

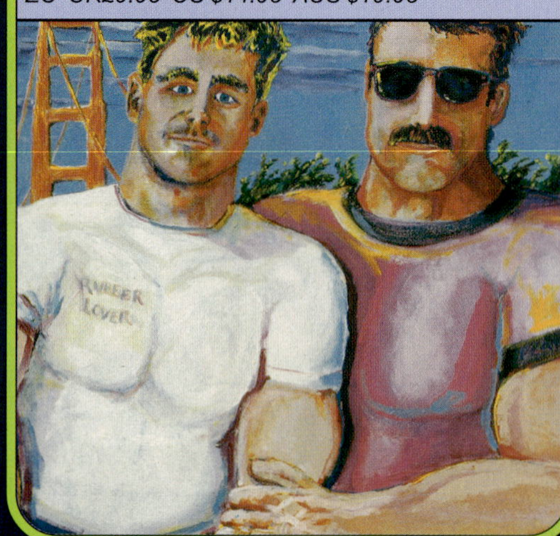

all illustrations are details

Hywel Williams
TOUCHLINE
– photographs

A classic collection of worked upon bodies in their prime – focussing upon the torso with its lyrical musculature and nipples, penises also figure prominently. His fine full colour studies of north London models have become a photographic legend.

(72 pages, 228 x 255mm, 64 colourplates)
ISBN 0 85449 293 3   medium format softback
EU UK£19.95 US $30   AUS $35

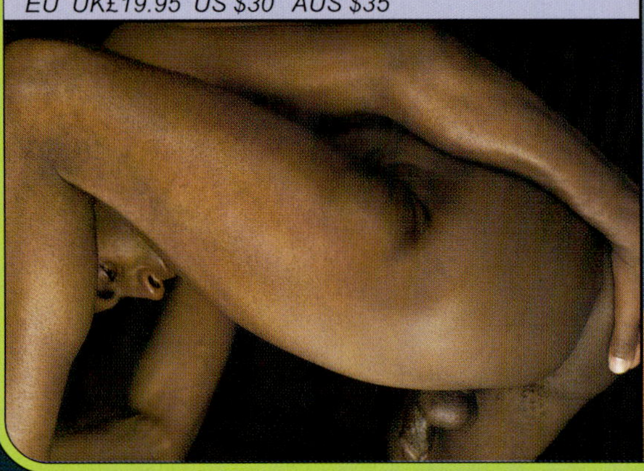

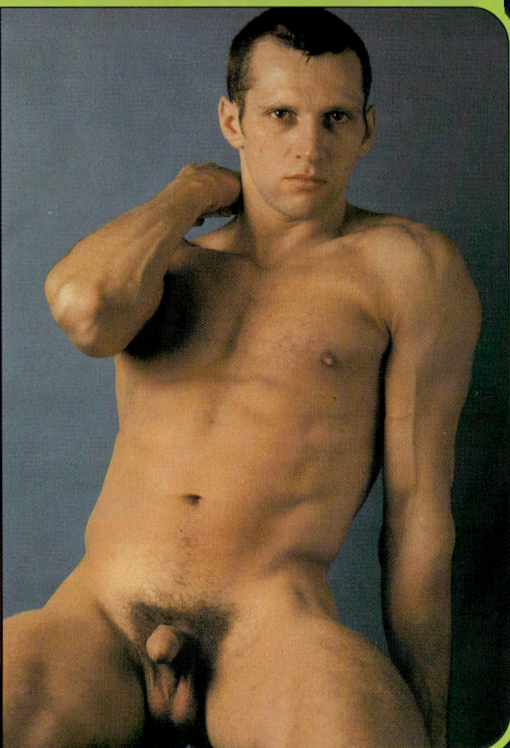

Michael Huhn
PHOTOS

Lean and muscled body-boys emerge from the street to flex and pose from downtown roofscapes immersed in the soaring Manhattan skyline. "There's plenty here to get hot and bothered about" – *HIM*
(64 pages, 305 x 245mm, 60 duotone plates)
ISBN 0 85449 173 2   large format softback
EU UK£9.95   AUS $19.95 not USA

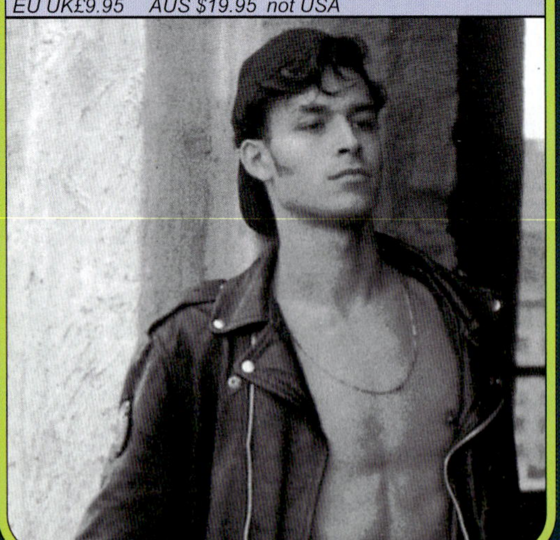

Don Pasquella
COMFORT OF DREAMS

Haunting photo images of naked male youth exploring raw desire in which the privacy of the model appears totally uninvaded, despite an ever-present rich sensuality.
(64 pages, 232 x 170mm, 61 duotone plates)
ISBN 0 85449 140 6   concise format softback
EU UK£10.95 US $14.95   AUS $29.95

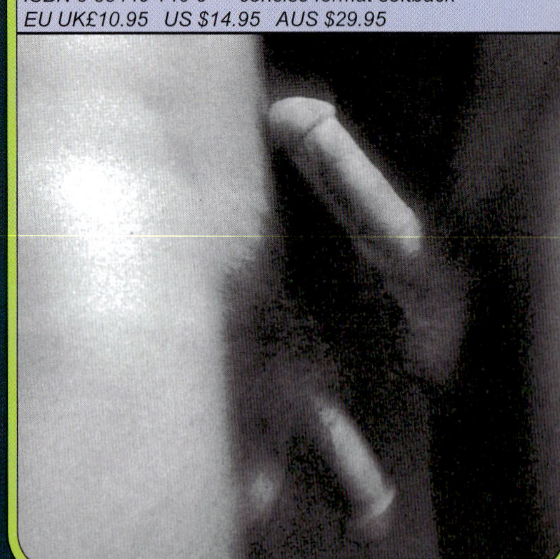

Sadao Hasegawa
SADAO HASEGAWA – paintings
Introduced by Frits Staal

From Japan comes this fabulous collection of gay erotic art. Hasegawa's work really is quite unique – like Tom of Finland, he has given the gay male world more classic iconic images which though thoroughly Japanese have become truly international. His work is both incredibly sexy and an amazing hybrid – influenced by major world cultures.
(80 pages, 305 x 245mm, 60 color plates)
ISBN 0 85449 226 7   large format softback
EU UK£19.95 US $29.95 AUS $39.95
reprinting FEB 2000

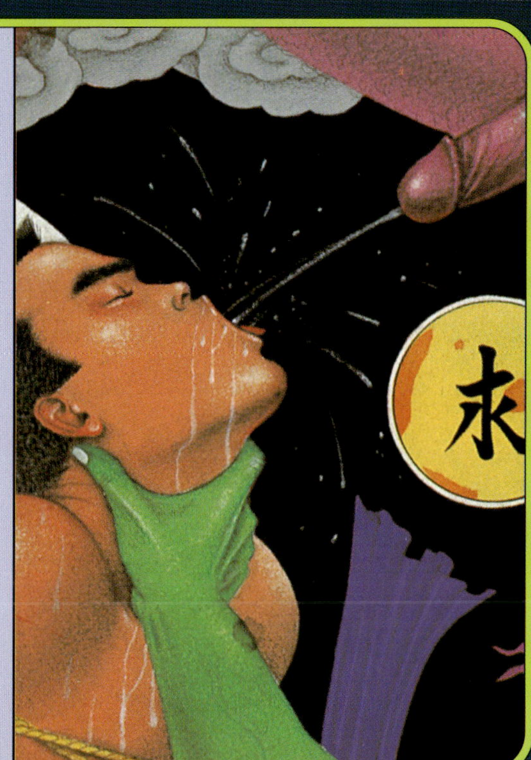

Kevin Lee
UNDERCURRENTS
These are basic photos of lovely lads. Jason likes his jockstrap, Chris likes his nipple rings, and Richard likes his dick! A collection of 14 models in various poses nude and otherwise on the beach, in the veldt, underwater, in the studio and in the bedroom.
(64 pages, 305 x 245mm, 60 duotone plates)
ISBN 0 85449 196 1   large format softback
EU UK£9.95 US $14.95 AUS $19.95

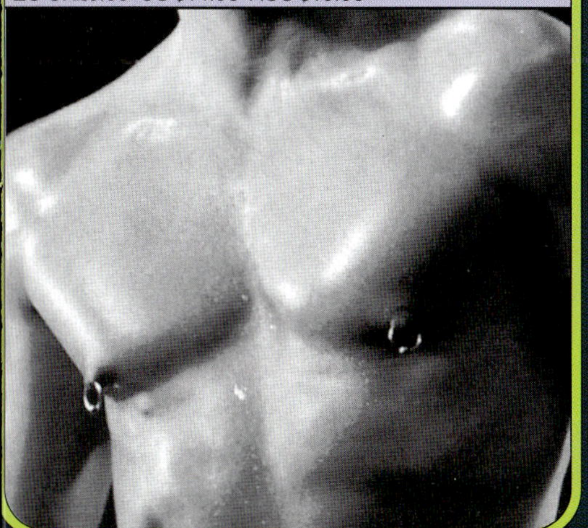

Don Whitman
MOUNTAIN MEN
An absolute classic of pure physique photography. Enthused with strong gay feeling these are photos of the most beautifully proportioned and body-sculpted males of 50s and 60s Western America, many posed with or without pouches on Rocky Mountain slopes.
(96 pages, 255 x 228mm, 8 color, 72 b/w plates)
ISBN 0 85449 148 1   medium format softback
EU UK£9.95 US $14.95 AUS $19.95

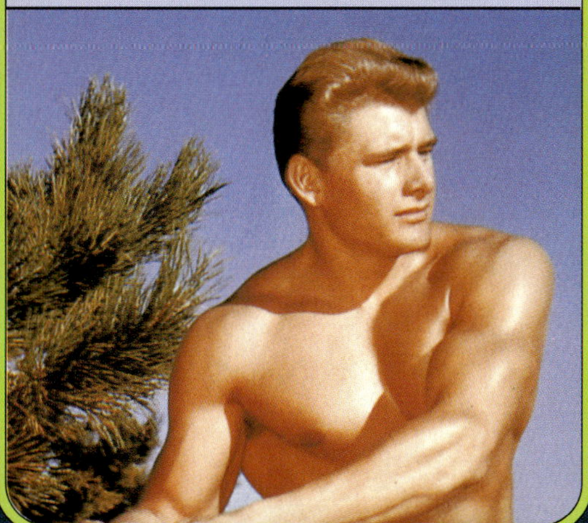

Roberto Gonzalez Fernandez
JOURNEYS

From Spain comes this striking collection of paintings reflecting a sensibility lying at the core of Spanish gay culture.

The artist excells at a photorealist style – homoerotic, thoughtful and moodful, these paintings with their blend of subtle coloration are totally about today.

(64 pages, 255 x 228mm, 39 color, 8 b/w plates
ISBN 0 85449 070 1   medium format softback
EU UK£9.95 US $ 14.95 AUS $19.95

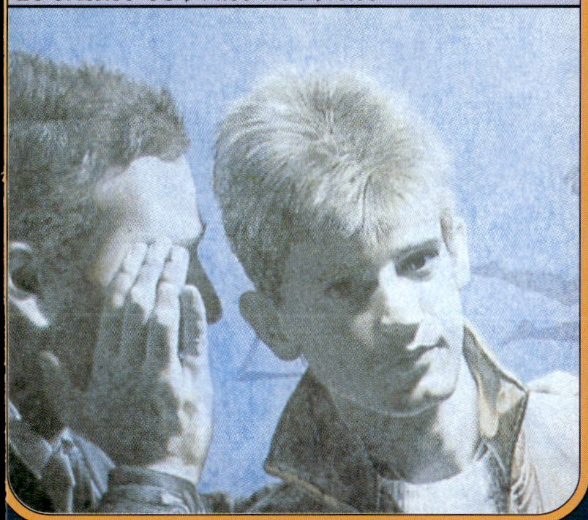

Douglas Blair Turnbaugh (ed)
PRIVATE : The Erotic Art of Duncan Grant

An intriguing and very sexy collection of Bloomsbury painter Duncan Grant's personal erotica. Often executed on mere scraps of paper they leave us in absolutely no doubt about his sexual desire. These small drawings can be very beautiful in their depiction of gay sex and also incredibly humorous.

(80 pages, 260 x 235mm, 36 color, 22 b/w plates)
ISBN 0 85449 099 X medium format hardback
EU UK£25.00 US $45.00 AUS $59.95

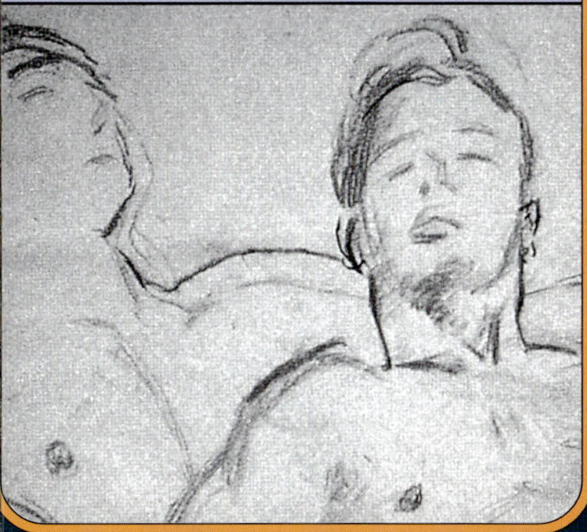

Nick Stanley
OUT IN ART

Five openly out gay artists of the 1980s, at a time of relative liberation, here display their varied work.

(64 pages, 200 x 200mm, 37 color plates)
ISBN 0 85449 027 2 concise format softback
EU UK£7.95 AUS $24.95 not USA

(also in hardback – see order form)

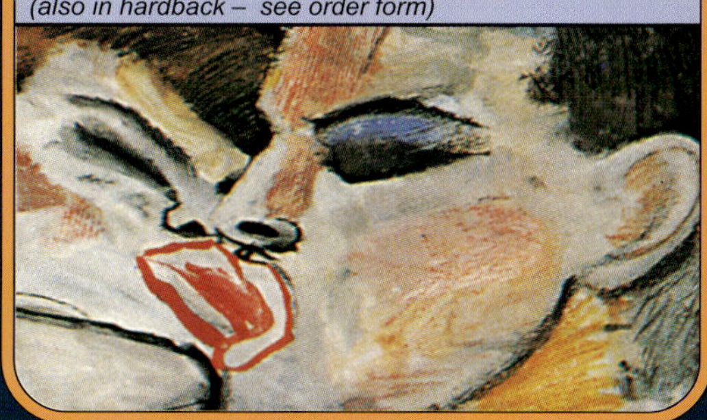

Philip Core
PAINTINGS

Core celebrated the ritz of modern urban gay life with all its contradictions from an open and proud gay stance.

(96 pages, 200 x 200mm, 40 color plates)
ISBN 0 907040 67 5   concise format hardback
EU UK£9.95 AUS $19.95   not USA

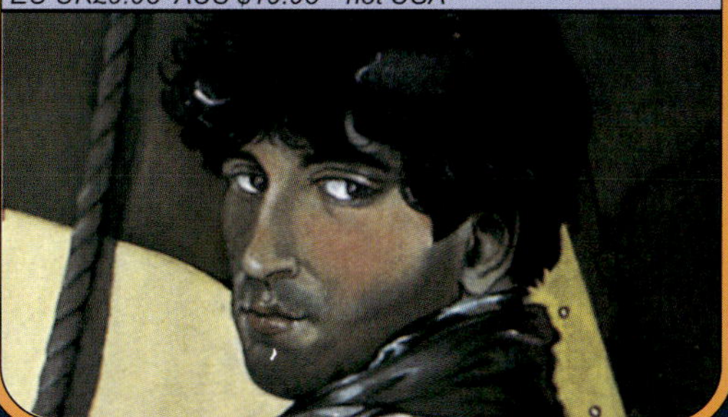

Mario Dubsky
TOM PILGRIM'S PROGRESS

Drawings that express the pain and suffering of gay consciousness under the heterosexual yoke.

(84 pages, 240 x 225mm, 64 b/w plates)
ISBN 0 907040 09 8 medium format softback
EU UK£9.95 US $17.50 AUS $14.95

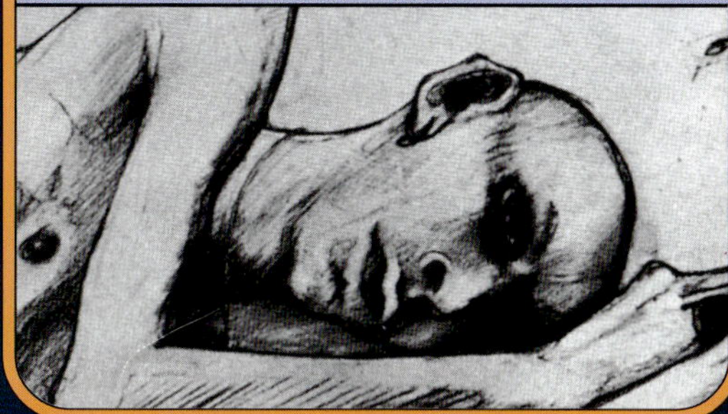

Ray Lawrence
MUSCLE ART

The artist defines the dream body in sensuous color; each muscle group is lovingly defined in classic pose.
(64 pages, 255 x 228mm, 40 color plates)
ISBN 0 85449 198 8   medium format softback
EU UK£9.95 US $14.95   AUS $19.95

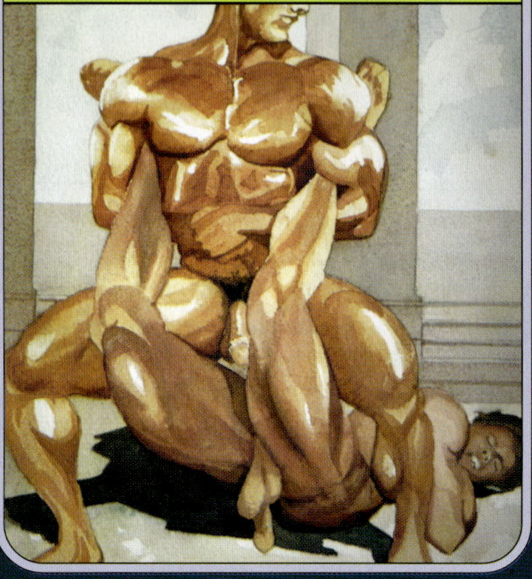

Douglas Simonson
HAWAII

A portfolio of drawings, paintings and etchings that bring alive the warmth and homosensuality of this beautiful place, above all featuring lovely young Hawaiian guys. Essentially a gay celebration of the male body, sun, sea and surf and wonderfully crafted by this highly talented artist.
(64 pages, 200 x 200mm, 40 color plates)
ISBN 0 85449 016 7   concise format softback
EU UK£8.95 US $17.50 AUS $24.95
(also in hardback – see order form)

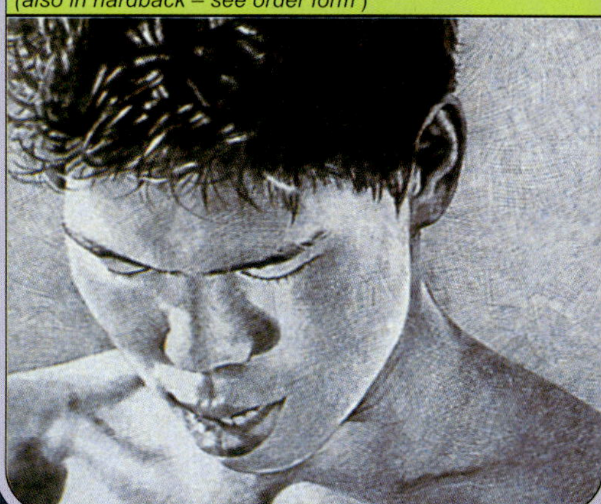

Greg Cloud
L.A. DREAMS

Bold, contemporary and uncompromising photo collection from the streets and gay clubs of Los Angeles. "Intense and passionate" – *Campaign*
(72 pages, 255 x 228mm, 60 color plates)
ISBN 0 85449 121 X   medium format softback
EU UK£9.95 US $14.95 AUS $19.95

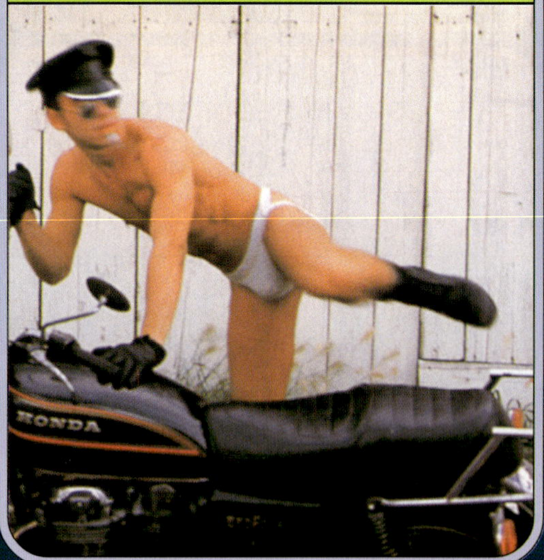

Della Grace
LOVE BITES

Rapidly established as a modern classic, this is the pioneering, ground-breaking book of lesbian photography. Della Grace broke the silence with this anthology of bold new lesbian images. Self-affirmation, self-definition, her queer sensibilty grapples with gender like no other contemporary photographer.
(72 pages, 255 x 228mm, 20 color, 40 d/t plates)
ISBN 0 85449 150 3   medium format softback
EU UK£9.95 US $14.95 AUS $19.95

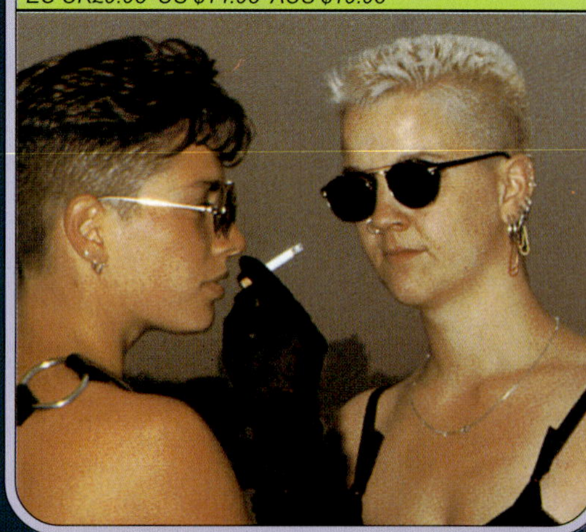

TRADE ORDERS – DISTRIBUTORS

North America
LPC / InBook, 1436 West Randolph St, Chicago, IL 60607, USA
phone: (312) 432 7650   fax: (312) 432 7603
Toll-Free Orders: *phone: 1 800 626 4330 / 1 800 243 0138*
fax: 1 800 334 3892

Australia & New Zealand
Bulldog Books, PO Box 300, Beaconsfield, NSW 2014
phone: (02) 9699 3507   fax: (02) 9699 3527

UK & Europe
Central Books, 99 Wallis Road, London E9 5LN, England
phone: 0181 986 4854 fax: 0181 533 5821

MAIL ORDER
DELIVERY ADDRESS (BLOCK CAPS PLEASE)
NAME ______________________________________
ADDRESS___________________________________
____
____
______________ POST CODE_________________

⊘   **PAYMENT METHOD** (IN UK POUNDS)
◯   CHEQUE / EUROCHEQUE / POSTAL ORDER
Cheques and Postal Orders made payable to:
Central Books Ltd
◯ VISA / MASTERCARD
◯ AMERICAN EXPRESS
I enclose payment to the value of UK £_____________
Signature____

CARD NUMBER ↓
____

CARD EXPIRY DATE ↓
____

Name & Address on card if different
from delivery address ↓
____
____
____
____

SEND YOUR COMPLETED ORDER FORM TO ↓

CENTRAL BOOKS, mail order
99 Wallis Road, London E9 5LN, England
fax: (44) 0181 533 5821
e-mail : mo@centralbooks.com

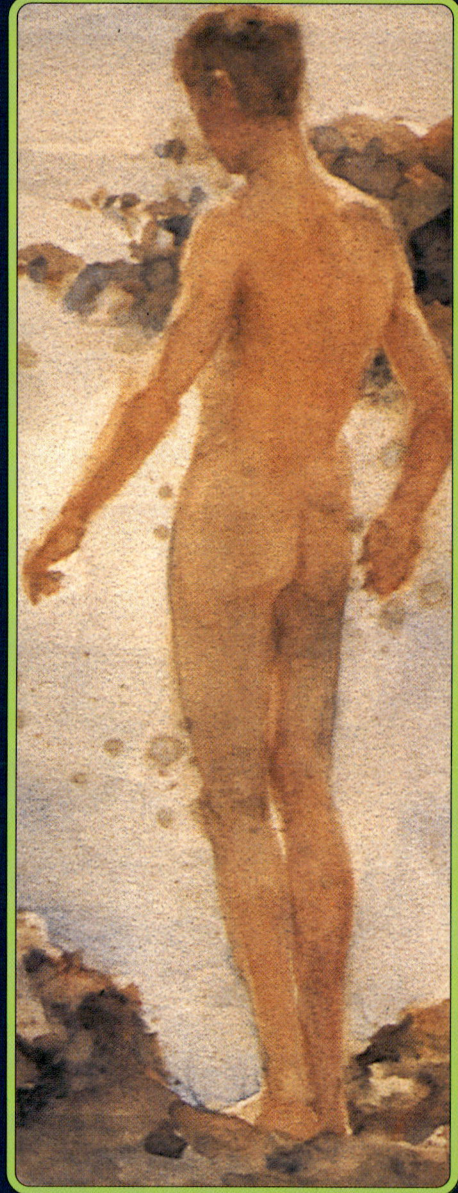

all illustrations are details